全国职业技能英语系列教材

总主编　童敬东
总顾问　陆松岩

职场综合英语教程

第二册
（第二版）

主　编　张　荣
副主编　史雯娜
编　者　陈　婧　易雅琼　袁　平
　　　　黄海燕　吴　翔

Vocational
Comprehensive
English-Training
Course

北京大学出版社
PEKING UNIVERSITY PRESS

图书在版编目(CIP)数据

职场综合英语教程. 第二册/张荣主编. —2版. —北京：北京大学出版社，2017.10
（全国职业技能英语系列教材）
ISBN 978-7-301-28879-5

Ⅰ.①职… Ⅱ.①张… Ⅲ.①英语–高等职业教育–教材 Ⅳ.①H319.39

中国版本图书馆CIP数据核字(2017)第250107号

书　　名	职场综合英语教程 第二册（第二版） ZHICHANG ZONGHE YINGYU JIAOCHENG DI-ER CE
著作责任者	张　荣　主编
责任编辑	李　娜
标准书号	ISBN 978-7-301-28879-5
出版发行	北京大学出版社
地　　址	北京市海淀区成府路205号　100871
网　　址	http://www.pup.cn　　新浪微博:@北京大学出版社
电子信箱	345014015@qq.com
电　　话	邮购部 62752015　发行部 62750672　编辑部 62759634
印刷者	北京宏伟双华印刷有限公司
经销者	新华书店 787毫米×1092毫米　16开本　8.75印张　280千字 2012年8月第1版 2017年10月第2版　2020年 7月第2次印刷
定　　价	39.00元

未经许可，不得以任何方式复制或抄袭本书之部分或全部内容。
版权所有，侵权必究
举报电话: 010-62752024　电子信箱: fd@pup.pku.edu.cn
图书如有印装质量问题，请与出版部联系，电话: 010-62756370

第二版前言

《职场综合英语教程》自2012年出版以来经历了五个春秋。在此期间,高等职业教育的规模、生源、教学方法发生了新的变化。甚至针对高职高专设计的"高等学校英语应用能力考试"大纲和题型也有了明显的变化。基于此,在北京大学出版社的积极策划下,《职场综合英语教程》原分册主编积极沟通,并征求使用教材师生的意见,决定对原教材进行修订。

本次修订的原则是减少课文单元,降低课文难度,采用牛津词典常用音标,适当增加与高职高专英语技能大赛及最新"高等学校英语应用能力考试"(B级)题型相关的练习。修订主要体现在以下几个方面:

1. 基础篇保留六个单元框架,但更换了难度较大的篇章,使修订后的课文更贴近学生的英语水平。此外,所有音标改用牛津词典音标,与学生在中学阶段所学音标保持一致,更便于学生课前预习和教师组织课堂教学。

2. 第一册最明显的变化是删除两个话题较偏的单元,使原来的八个单元变成现在的六个单元。另外,与基础篇的修订方法相同,对所有生词采用牛津词典音标进行标注。

3. 第二册最明显的变化是压缩了原有单元,并对个别课文进行了降低难度的处理。与此同时,我们还对书中练习进行了修订,压缩或删除了部分实用性较弱的练习。这样做的目的是使本书内容更接近学生的学习能力,便于教师组织教学和调动学生的学习积极性。

4. 第三册秉承前几册的修订原则,对原书八个单元内容进行了压缩,删除了难度较大的篇章,保留了与职场关系度较高且难度适中的单元内容。所有生词的音标参照《牛津高阶英汉双解词典》(第七版)进行标注。此外,我们还对写作部分进行了必要的修订,剔除了与前几册重复的内容,增加了与职业技能大赛有关的话题。

五年来的教学实践证明,《职场综合英语教程》是一套严格按照国家职业教育目标和要求精心设计的高职高专公共英语教材,选材新颖,话题丰富,满足高职高专英语教学的实际需要。我们相信,修订后的这套教材更加符合高职高专教育对公共英语的教学要求,更加适合学习者的学习水平,更加有助于学生未来的职业发展。

编者
2017年7月

第一版前言

职业化已经成为高职高专教育最显著的特征。增加实训、强调动手能力、采用"订单式"培养模式是其主要特色。在这种背景下,按照传统的教学方法进行基础课教学已经不容置疑的受到了挑战。就目前情况论,高职高专的基础课教学必须践行"以服务为宗旨,以就业为导向"的专业建设指导思想。在课程建设以及基础课教学内容中,必须结合学生的专业需求,有意识地融入与职场相关联的知识。

根据教育部《高职高专英语教育课程教学基本要求》的精神,联合国家级示范高职院校和骨干高职院校的一线教师,在充分调查现有高职高专英语教材的基础上,结合高职英语教学的未来发展趋势,在"安徽省高职高专外语教研会"的组织及北京大学出版社的支持下,编写了本套《职场综合英语教程》,并被列入普通高等教育"十二五"规划教材。

本套教程分为基础篇、第一册、第二册和第三册,共四册。

基础篇 主要针对英语基础比较薄弱的学生,融入了对音标的训练,旨在帮助这部分学生巩固英语的基础知识,为后续课程的学习奠定必要的基础。

第一册 主要涉及西方文化和日常生活,内容涵盖西方名人、青年旅馆、主题公园、肥皂剧、网上购物等。鲜活的内容、生活化的主题,有利于学生顺利融入大学生活,同时也有助于培养学生对英语学习的兴趣,为今后的职业化过渡打下坚实基础。

第二册 主要涉及求职以及职业素养培养等主题,如求职、自主创业、职场中人际交往和做好服务、科技与生活、名人的成功与失败等。另外,本册内容与职场文化的有机融合有利于学生对未来职业规划形成初步的认识。

第三册 从职场生活出发,针对高职学生可能遇到的职场活动进行设计,内容包括机场接待、银行服务、汽车制造等。内容难度适中,选材谨慎,真正做到通识化与职场化有机统筹,有助于学生以后进一步学习相关的专业英语。

本套教材的内容主要分为六个方面:听说、阅读、语法、应用文写作、文化速递与拓展词汇。

听说部分 践行任务型教学的指导思想,强调能听懂简单对话,能记录关键词,能就所给事物说出英语名称,或进行角色分工,完成简单对话。这部分设计了热身环节,通过比较容易完成的任务,帮助学生尽快进入相关主题的学习。而角色扮演部分则试

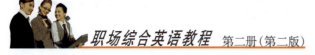

图充分调动学生的想象力和创造力,按照角色分工完成任务。听说部分还设计了听写内容,旨在培养学生听懂并记录关键词的能力。

阅读部分 由两篇相关主题的文章组成,其中第一篇为主要文章,教师应该进行精深讲解;第二篇属于附加文章,教师可以把它作为泛读教材使用。目的是让学生在阅读过程中完成对该主题的英语核心词汇的巩固和学习,同时深刻理解英语的语句结构。

语法部分 旨在夯实高职高专学生的语法基础,改善语法能力薄弱的现状,同时结合"高等学校英语应用能力考试"要求,对一些考试技巧进行精解,真正做到融会贯通,为提高英语综合能力打下良好基础。

写作部分 紧扣职场,重在应用文的写作。提供较规范的写作模式与常用句型供学生参考,通过实际的操练让学生进一步熟悉并掌握多种应用文的写作。

文化速递 是本套教材的特色之一。是针对单元主题的拓展性学习资料,可以帮助学生开阔视野、拓展知识面,提高综合人文素养。

词汇部分 依据大纲要求,课文中涉及的生词均分级标出。标★为A级词汇,标☆为超纲词汇。方便教师把握教学重点,也方便学生分级掌握词汇,逐步晋级。

配有教学课件 每个单元针对不同的主题都有话题的进一步延伸,有利于教师进行拓展教学。丰富授课内容,活跃课堂气氛,激发学生的学习兴趣。

本套教材得到教育部高等学校高职高专英语类专业教学指导委员会的悉心指导,由教指委秘书长牛健博士和副主任委员丁国声教授担任总顾问,由安徽新华学院外国语学院院长任静生教授担任总主编,国家示范性高等职业院校芜湖职业技术学院、安徽水利水电职业技术学院、安徽职业技术学院、安庆职业技术学院等院校的英语教学专家负责编写任务;明尼苏达大学商业管理Brian Meyer博士以及天津外国语大学等院校的专家为此套教材的出版倾注了大量的心血;其他参编人员及编辑老师们也付出了巨大的努力,在此谨向他们表示衷心的感谢。

高职高专英语教学任重道远,教材建设未有止境。本套教材的出版旨在探索新形势下高职高专英语教学的一条教学新路。缺点与不足之处在所难免,衷心希望得到专家学者的批评指正,听到广大师生的改进意见。

编者
2012年12月

Contents

| Unit 1 | Job Hunting ··· 1 |

Part Ⅰ　Listening and Speaking / 2
Part Ⅱ　Reading / 5
　　　　Text A　5 Sure-fire Ways to Mess up a Job Interview / 6
　　　　Text B　Challenging Job Market in China / 10
Part Ⅲ　Strategies: 听力解析 / 15
Part Ⅳ　Applied Writing: Résumé(简历) / 17
Part Ⅴ　Cultural Express: Job Hunting Tips / 19

| Unit 2 | Interesting Jobs ··· 22 |

Part Ⅰ　Listening and Speaking / 23
Part Ⅱ　Reading / 27
　　　　Text A　Event Planning: Wedding / 27
　　　　Text B　Premarital Counseling / 32
Part Ⅲ　Strategies: 词汇解析 / 35
Part Ⅳ　Applied Writing: Contract (合同) / 40
Part Ⅴ　Cultural Express: Trying Different Jobs vs. Taking a Long Term Career / 43

| Unit 3 | Business on Campus ··· 46 |

Part Ⅰ　Listening and Speaking / 47
Part Ⅱ　Reading / 50
　　　　Text A　To Be the Next Millionaire / 51
　　　　Text B　Money Making Schemes / 55
Part Ⅲ　Strategies: 翻译解析 / 58
Part Ⅳ　Applied Writing: Specification (说明书) / 60
Part Ⅴ　Cultural Express: Tips on Starting an E-Business / 61

Unit 4　Customer Service ··· **64**

  Part Ⅰ　Listening and Speaking / 65
  Part Ⅱ　Reading / 69
    Text A　The Greatest Customer Service Story Ever Told / 69
    Text B　Rules for Good Customer Service / 74
  Part Ⅲ　Strategies: 写作解析 / 77
  Part Ⅳ　Applied Writing: Complaint Letter (投诉信) / 80
  Part Ⅴ　Cultural Express: Wal-Mart Business Culture / 81

Unit 5　Culture Shock ··· **84**

  Part Ⅰ　Listening and Speaking / 85
  Part Ⅱ　Reading / 90
    Text A　Disney Culture Shock / 91
    Text B　How to Handle Business Culture Shock / 95
  Part Ⅲ　Strategies: 阅读解析(一) / 100
  Part Ⅳ　Applied Writing: Welcome Speech/Letter (欢迎词) / 107
  Part Ⅴ　Cultural Express: Cross-Cultural Differences / 109
          Travel in China / 110

Unit 6　Technology and Life ··· **113**

  Part Ⅰ　Listening and Speaking / 114
  Part Ⅱ　Reading / 118
    Text A　How Has Technology Changed Our Lives / 118
    Text B　How Did the iPad Change Our Lives? / 122
  Part Ⅲ　Strategies: 阅读解析(二) / 125
  Part Ⅳ　Applied Writing: Farewell Speech/Letter (欢送词) / 128
  Part Ⅴ　Cultural Express：What Is Intercultural Communication？/ 130
          German or Global? / 130

Unit 1

Job Hunting

Learning Objectives:

You are able to:

☞ Design a resume

☞ Write an application letter

You are suggested to:

☞ Recognize the English terms for different positions

☞ Be familiar with some well-known companies

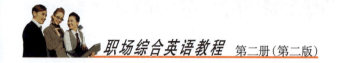

Part I Listening and Speaking

Warm-up

Task 1

Directions: Do you know their Chinese meanings? Try to say something about them.

| blouse | dress | high-heeled shoes | handbag | tie |
| briefcase | watch | necklace | lighter | tie-clip |

(1) (2) (3) (4) (5) (6) (7) (8) (9) (10)

Task 2

Directions: Work with your partner and match the following Chinese phrases with their English equivalents.

推荐信 ☆
成绩单 ☆
毕业证书 ☆
初级工作 ☆
团队工作能力 ☆
推荐人 ☆
学位证书 ☆
简历 ☆

★ school transcript
★ teamwork ability
★ entry-level work
★ a letter of recommendation
★ graduate certificate
★ résumé
★ diploma
★ referee

Oral Practice

Task 1

Directions: Read the dialogue and answer the following questions.

Ivy: Which school are you attending?
Alice: I am attending Hebei University of Technology.
Ivy: When will you graduate from that university?
Alice: This coming July.
Ivy: What degree will you receive?

Alice: I will receive a Bachelor's degree.
Ivy: What is your major?
Alice: My major is Business Administration.
Ivy: How have you been getting on with your studies so far?
Alice: I have been doing quite well at college. According to the academic records I've achieved so far, I am confident that I will receive my Bachelor of Business Administration degree this coming July.

1. When will Alice graduate from that university?
   ☐ This July.   ☐ Next July.
2. What is Alice's major?
   ☐ Business Management.   ☐ Business Administration.
3. Why is Alice so confident with herself?
   ☐ She has achieved a good academic standing at college.
   ☐ She will receive the Bachelor of Business Administration degree.

Task 2

Directions: Suppose you are the interviewee for the position of computer technician in a company, your partner is an interviewer. Use the information in the following résumé and role-play an interview with your partner. Then reverse roles and do it again.

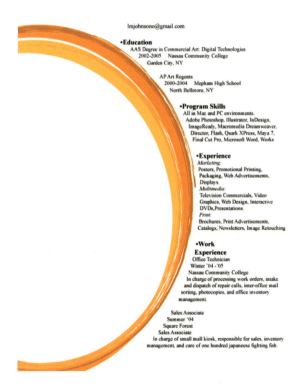

Listening Practice

Task 1

Directions: Listen to an interview and tick (√) in the box at the end of the correct answer.

1. The age of the interviewee is_____.
    A. 24 years old ☐
    B. 25 years old ☐
    C. 26 years old ☐
2. The interviewee was born in_____.
    A. Beijing ☐
    B. Nanjing ☐
    C. Tianjin ☐
3. The interviewee is now living in_____.
    A. 606 Zhongguancun Road, Apt 802, Beijing ☐
    B. 660 Zhongguancun Road, Apt 820, Beijing ☐
    C. 666 Zhongguancun Road, Apt 802, Beijing ☐
4. The interviewee is_____.
    A. single ☐
    B. married ☐
    C. divorced ☐
5. In the interviewee's family there are_____.
    A. her parents, her elder sister and her ☐
    B. her parents, her younger sister and her ☐
    C. her parents, her elder brother and her ☐

Task 2

Directions: In this section you will hear a recorded short passage. The passage will be read three times. You are required to put the missing words or phrases in the numbered blanks according to what you hear.

There are (1)_____ other types of vocational schools in Germany. The first one is the (2)_____ School, a full-time secondary vocational school. These schools do not (3)_____ any tuition fees. The course at this type of school lasts 1–3 years. This type of education prepares the students for special (4)_____ trainings. Students can also get a (5)_____ graduation at the school. The second additional (6)_____ of German vocational schools is the (7)_____ School, a full-time or part-time post-secondary vocational school, and also most often a (8)_____ school. Only graduates of a vocational school, with (often) at least 1 year (9)_____ experience after graduation, are permitted to attend this type of school. The (10)_____ at a Training school lasts 1–2 years for full-time students and 2–4 years for part-time students.

• Unit 1 Job Hunting •

Task 3

Directions: Listen to a conversation and work with your partner to fill in the blanks of the form given below.

```
              Candidate Form
1. Name of Candidate : _____
2. Age : _____
3. Sex : _____
4. The position of the job you want to apply for : _____
5. How did you get the information about this job : _____
```

Part II Reading

Text A

Before Reading:

Seeing the following pictures, can you tell what they do for a living?

5 Sure-fire Ways to Mess up a Job Interview

Whether it's your first interview or just another one of many, there's always a chance that you'll mess up. Employers are aware of the fact that interviewees unavoidably experience huge pressure and the stress can cause them to make mistakes. There are, however, some things which can instantly put off an employer and ruin your chances of getting hired, regardless of what your résumé has to offer.

Everyone has certain habits, which is quite normal, but you should try to stop them during a job interview. Biting your nails due to nervousness won't do too much harm, but picking your nose or other body parts really isn't recommended. You may not notice you have these bad habits, so try a practice interview with a friend or family member who can identify any bad habits for you to eliminate.

Avoid bad mouthing and complaining about previous employers, even if it was the reason you left your job. Pushing the blame doesn't make you look good, rather it creates the image that you're a troublesome employee. Think of another reason to provide your interviewer with when questioned about previous jobs. Simply saying the job wasn't for you might be enough.

Getting your interviewer's name and title wrong can cause offense and certainly won't win you any bonus points. If you're unsure about their names and titles, it's best to leave them out. Avoid piling additional pressure onto yourself, just concentrate on remaining calm and in control.

Nothing gives off a worst impression than showing up to a job interview late—it shows lack of responsibility and little motivation. Aim to arrive at least fifteen minutes early and give yourself extra time if you're unsure of the exact location.

In some cases, unexpected situations can cause you to be late for an interview or unable to attend and employers do understand this can happen. If there's been an accident on the motorway or a family member falls sick, call and apologize, explain the situation and reschedule the interview. Always make sure you tell them you're still interested in the position and that you regret the situation has arisen at an unfortunate time.

Confidence is a positive quality which can help you do well in the job interview but arrogance is not. Arrogance can really discourage a potential employer from hiring you as you'll appear difficult to manage and unlikely to follow instruction. Make sure you're eager and attentive during your interview and show that you're listening by making eye contact with them.

Avoid using coarse language inside and outside of the interview room. There's plenty of time for those things once you've been hired...

Unit 1 Job Hunting

New Words

(标★为A级词汇,标☆为超纲词汇)

pressure	/ˈpreʃə/	n.	压(力);压力;气压(或血压);压(迫)感
stress	/stres/	n.	强调;重音;压力;重力
offer	/ˈɒfə/	v.	提供,给予;提出,提议;出价,开价;表示愿意
recommend	/rekəˈmend/	v.	推荐;劝告;使显得吸引人;托付
★eliminate	/ɪˈlɪmɪneɪt/	v.	消除;根除(尤指不需要之物)
previous	/ˈpriːvɪəs/	adj.	先前的;以前的;过早的;(时间上)稍前的
employee	/emplɔɪˈiː, emˈplɔɪiː/	n.	雇工,雇员,职工
offense	/əˈfens/	n.	犯罪,违反;冒犯,触怒;攻击
bonus	/ˈbəʊnəs/	n.	奖金,额外津贴;红利,额外股息;退职金;额外令人高兴的事情
pile	/paɪl/	n.	桩;一堆;绒头;摞
		v.	堆起;堆叠;放置;装入;蜂拥,拥挤
situation	/sɪtjʊˈeɪʃ(ə)n/	n.	(人的)情况;局面,形势,处境,位置;[心理学]情境
arise	/əˈraɪz/	v	产生;出现;起身,起立;起源于,产生于
★discourage	/dɪsˈkʌrɪdʒ/	v.	使气馁;使沮丧;阻碍;劝阻
★potential	/pə(ʊ)ˈtenʃ(ə)l/	adj.	潜在的,有可能的

Phrases and Expressions

mess up	弄乱,弄糟
be aware of	知道,意识到
concentrate on	专心于,把思想集中于;将……集中于

Proper Names

Sure-fire 确切的
5 Sure-fire Ways to Mess up a Job Interview 五种做法肯定砸了你的面试

Exercises

I. Reading Comprehension

Directions: Circle the right answer for the following questions.

1. Why do interviewees often make mistakes in the interviews?
    A. Because it is their first interview.
    B. Because the employers give them a lot of pressure.
    C. Because they have huge pressure from the job interview and become very nervous.
    D. Because they don't prepare the CV well.
2. Which one is not the behavior the interviewees should avoid in an interview?
    A. Biting the nails.
    B. Being aware of bad habits.
    C. Picking the nose.
    D. Pushing the blame.
3. If the interviewees are unsure about the interviewer's names and titles, _____.
    A. they can ask them before the interview
    B. they should keep calm and be in control
    C. they should concentrate on them
    D. they can give themselves a lot of pressure
4. Which should the interviewees not do if they have an unexpected reason for being late?
    A. Inform the interviewers of the situation.
    B. Tell the interviewers you're still interested in the position.
    C. Call the interviewers and ask them to wait for you.
    D. Regret the situation has arisen at an unfortunate time.
5. The interviewees should not be _____ in the interview.
    A. eager
    B. arrogant
    C. attentive
    D. confident

II. True or False

Directions: Decide whether the following statements are true or false according to the text. Write "T" if the statement is true and "F" if it is false.

_____ 1. The applicants should practice the interview, so they can be relaxed before the real one.

_____ 2. The previous employers are the reason for the applicants leaving their former jobs.

_____ 3. Getting the applicant's name and title will not do any help in the interview.

_____ 4. Being late to an interview shows lack of responsibility and little motivation.
_____ 5. Once the applicants get out of the interview room, they can express opposing views.

III. Word Usage

Directions: Complete each of the following sentences with the correct form of the italicized word given in the brackets.

1. Heavy Metal music really _____ *(arise)* in the late 60s.
2. I must _____ *(concentrate)* on my work now.
3. _____ *(pressure)* of time meant that he became adept at writing in railway carriages.
4. Who _____ *(be in control)* of the project?
5. The _____ *(situation)* suddenly became tense.
6. The library is now _____ *(offer)* computer service.
7. What about the _____ *(bonus)* in your company?
8. John was _____ *(eager)* to invite us to the party.

IV. Blank Filling

Directions: Translate the Chinese part of the following sentences with the correct form of the words or expressions in the box.

| mess up | be aware of | concentrate on | eliminate |
| previous | offense | pile | recommend |

1. After the fun he's had during the holidays, the boy can't _____ his school work. (集中注意力)
2. Can we ever _____ poverty from the world?（消除）
3. If I _____, I would probably be fired.（搞砸了）
4. The teacher examined the students on the _____ lesson.（前面的）
5. As time went on, people came to _____ the seriousness of China's population size.（认识到）
6. _____ the leaves in the corner of the yard.（堆）
7. Because it was his first _____, the punishment wasn't too severe.（初犯）
8. Can you _____ him to the manager?（推荐）

V. Translation

Directions: Put the following English sentences into Chinese.

1. Your advice will make my job-hunting a lot easier in the future.
2. The interviewer will judge the interviewee's attitude by asking the motivation of the interviewee.
3. He was very nervous during his first job interview, which was understandable.
4. My résumé shows that I have the right qualifications for the job.
5. I learned of the position through a newspaper advertisement.

Text B

Before Reading:

1. What are you going to do after graduation?
2. What kind of job do you expect to get and why?

Challenging Job Market in China

When Chelsea Cai graduated from university this year (2008), she had no idea the job market would be quite so depressing. Over the past three months, Cai, a graduate of Shanghai Jiao Tong University, has sent out over 50 résumés to different companies and has managed to land interviews with seven. So far, Cai, a food science and engineering major, has received one offer as a research assistant from a company that specializes in producing MSG, but has dismissed the monthly salary of RMB 2,500 as too low.

Cai is waiting to hear the results from another recent interview with a state-owned organic food producer, but she, like many of her peers, is getting increasingly frustrated.

"I've had enough of job hunting. I'm sending out résumés every day and am getting no replies, and it is just one disappointment after another. I was not prepared for this when I got out of school," says Cai.

Cai is one of 6.1 million students who will graduate from Chinese universities this year, an increase from the 5.6 million students who graduated in 2008 and nearly six times as many as in 2000. State sources predict that, by 2011, the number of Chinese university graduates will reach 7.6 million. University graduates have been facing difficulties in finding jobs for years. The problem doesn't result only from economic slowdown or too many people holding university degrees, but is due to a variety of different factors.

First, not only are there fewer jobs available because of the economic slowdown, but widespread cutbacks means there are more experienced people in the market who are competing for the same jobs as fresh graduates than in previous years.

Second, industries that have a high demand for workers have a comparatively low educational and skills requirement, and pay much lower wages. China's 9 to 10 percent economic growth in recent years has relied on industries that use laborers with low technical skills rather than university graduates. The nation's industrial structure cannot absorb so many university graduates; it has a greater demand for migrant workers instead.

Third, there are considerable differences in the development levels between the country's coastal region and inland, western areas. Most graduates seek jobs in the big cities in China's eastern regions, where the employment market is already relatively crowded.

Generating enough jobs for the masses of eager young students emerging from the country's universities has been a chief concern of the country's top decision makers for years. Since 1999, the number of college graduate students in China has grown by approximately 30 percent a year; as a result, the job market has been unable to keep pace with the surge of graduates entering each year.

New Words

（标★为A级词汇,标☆为超纲词汇）

★depressing	/dɪˈpresɪŋ/	adj.	令人忧愁的,使人沮丧的；使情绪低落的 (depress v.)
offer	/ˈɒfə/	n.	提议；出价,开价
★assistant	/əˈsɪst(ə)nt/	n.	助手,助理
dismiss	/dɪsˈmɪs/	v.	解雇,把……免职；遣散,解散（队伍等）；驳回,拒绝受理；搁置
organic	/ɔːˈɡænɪk/	adj.	有机（体）的；有组织的,系统的；器官的；根本的
cutback	/ˈkʌtbæk/	n.	削减,缩减
structure	/ˈstrʌktʃə/	n.	结构；构造；建筑物；体系
★absorb	/əbˈzɔːb, -ˈsɔːb/	v.	吸收（液体、气体等）；吸引（注意）；吞并,合并；忍受,承担（费用）
migrant	/ˈmaɪɡr(ə)nt/	n.	候鸟；移居者,移民；随季节迁移的工作者；迁移动物
		adj.	移居的；流浪的
generate	/ˈdʒenəreɪt/	v.	形成,造成；产生物理反应；产生（后代）；引起
approximately	/əˈprɒksɪmətlɪ/	adv.	近似地,大约
surge	/sɜːdʒ/	n.	汹涌；大浪,波涛

Phrases and Expressions

food science and engineering major	食品工程专业
MSG: Monosodium glutamate	味精
emerge from	来自
keep pace with	跟上,赶上

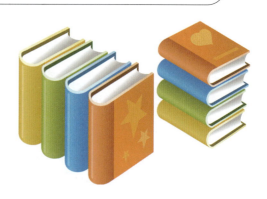

Unit 1 Job Hunting

Exercises

I. Summary

Directions: Fill in the blanks with the appropriate words according to your understanding.

　　The job market in China has been (1) _____ to keep pace with the surge of graduates (2) _____ each year. University graduates have been facing (3) _____ in job hunting for years. A lot of factors (4) _____ this problem: First, many (5) _____ people in the job market are competing for the same jobs with the (6) _____. Second, industries have a great demand for workers who have a lower educational and technical (7) _____, and pay much lower wages than graduates. Third, different regions and (8) _____ have different job markets. Most graduates have met more competitions in some big cities in China's (9) _____ regions. This is a serious problem for the country's top (10) _____ to solve.

II. Reading Comprehension

Directions: Circle the right answer for the following questions.

1. Which one is not true about Chelsea Cai?
    A. She was graduated from Shanghai Jiao Tong University.
    B. She was still confident about job hunting after graduation.
    C. She was waiting for the results from a state-owned organic food producer.
    D. She had attended recruitment fairs when she was in the university.
2. Which one is not the reason that university graduates face many difficulties in hunting jobs?
    A. Economic slowdown.
    B. Many competitors.
    C. Fewer jobs available.
    D. High job requirements.
3. Why do industries use laborers rather than university graduates?
    A. They have enough technical skills.
    B. They are paid much lower wages.
    C. They have enough technical background.
    D. They are more experienced.
4. Which is not the popular place for most graduates seeking jobs?
    A. Eastern regions.　　　　B. Coastal region.
    C. Western areas.　　　　　D. Developed areas.
5. Which one is true according to the passage?
    A. Recently the country's top decision makers are aware of the problem.
    B. The serious situation of job hunting frustrates the university graduates.
    C. The university graduates are more competitive than the workers in the job market.
    D. The job market is keeping pace with the wave of graduates entering the workforce.

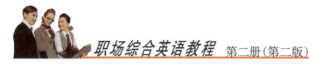

III. Vocabulary & Structures

Directions: Fill in the blanks with the proper words or expressions in the box.

| assistant | dismiss | surge | cutback |
| absorb | migrant | approximately | generate |

1. The way animals _____ nutrition(营养) from food can be quite different from human beings'.
2. In consequence of your bad work I am forced to _____ you.
3. The people attending the convention also _____ more business in the hotel's restaurants, bars and shops.
4. The gates opened and the crowd _____ forward.
5. People are concerned about the _____ in welfare programs.
6. _____ workers move from country to country in search of work.
7. An _____ one day a week would ease my workload.
8. Our English teacher is _____ in her forties.

IV. Translation

Directions: Put the following English sentences into Chinese.

1. They also let students know about job openings and job recruitment fairs.
2. My major subject is accounting and my minor subject is foreign trade.
3. Competition has forced out many small firms.
4. The job, for a university graduate, is one of the most concerning issues today.
5. Gain a distinct professional advantage in a competitive job market.

Unit 1　Job Hunting

Part III　Strategies

听力解析

听力理解分为问题、对话和短文听写三个部分。问题、对话部分共10个单项选择，每道题后附4个备选答案，短文听写部分共5题填空。

一、地点题

【试题特点】地点题提问的是对话发生的地点，常用的提问方式有：

Where does the conversation most probably take place?

Where does this conversation most likely occur?

Where are the two speakers?

【答题技巧】地点题的解答需要抓住与特定地点相关的常用词语。这类题目的对话中一般不会提到具体场所，问题往往要求根据对话内容推测出谈话场所或某人的去向。考生要注意抓取信息词，即与特定地点相关的最常用词语。

其次，考生需要熟悉常考的地点和不同场景下人们的谈话用语，这对做好地点题很有帮助。

【典型例题】

【例1】　　A) At a clinic.　　　B) In a supermarket.

　　　　　C) At a restaurant.　　D) In an ice cream shop.

W: I'll have the steak, French fries, and let's see, chocolate ice cream for dessert.

M: Oh, oh, you know these things will ruin your health, too much fat and sugar, how about ordering some vegetables and fruit instead?

Q: Where does the conversation most probably take place?

【解析】从四个选项中可以看出，本题是一道地点题。在对话中出现了该题的关键词 dessert 和 ordering，因此可以判断这一对话应当发生在餐馆里面。

二、人物关系或身份职业题

【试题特点】

1. 对人物关系的提问

   人物关系题常用的提问方式有：

   What's the probable relationship between the two speakers?

2. 对人物职业的提问

   身份职业题常用的提问方式有：

   Who is the man/the woman?

【答题技巧】

在解答人物关系和身份职业题时，一定要注意双方的称呼语。对话中的称呼语往往会直接暴露出说话人的身份或说话双方的关系,比如Mr.一词就表明对方很可能是自己的上级或老师。

同时要善于捕捉关键词及人物语气。解答这类试题,不但要熟悉体现某种人物关系或某种职业的相关词汇,而且要注意说话人的语气和态度,比如师生之间、夫妻之间、家长与孩子之间以及老板与员工之间的说话方式和语气均有自己的特点。

在短对话部分常考的职业身份有:

教授(professor)、秘书(secretary)、医生(doctor)、老板(boss)、服务员(waiter/waitress)、主人(host/hostess)、修理工(repairer)、管道工/水暖工(plumber)、电工(electrician)、家庭角色(husband/wife/son/daughter/girlfriend...)

短对话部分涉及的人物关系包括:

夫妻(husband—wife)、父子(father—son)、母子(mother—son)、师生(teacher—student)、同学(schoolmate/classmate)、同事(colleague)、老板与秘书(boss—secretary)、雇主与雇员(employer—employee)、医生与病人(doctor—patient)、服务员与顾客(waiter/waitress—customer)、主人与客人(host/hostess—guest)、警察与司机(policeman—driver)、管理员与借阅者(librarian—reader)、房东与租房者(landlord/landlady—tenant)

【典型例题】

【例2】　　A) A bank clerk.　　B) A secretary.　　C) A landlady.　　D) A doctor.

M: According to your ad. in this morning's paper, you have an apartment for rent.

W: Yes, I have. It's on the second floor. Would you like to have a look? Come this way, please.

Q: Who is the woman?

【解析】从四个选项看,该题提问的是身份职业。从对话中出现的关键词是an apartment for rent和ad.分析,录音中出现的男士和女士的关系应当是房东和租客的关系,因此这位女士应当是房东。

三、数字计算题

【试题特点】

数字计算题常见的提问方式有:

What time...?

How far/long...?

How much/many...?

数字计算题一般涉及时间和价钱的运算。

1. 对活动发生时间的提问。在通常情况下,该类试题一般不会直接告诉我们问题中所问的时间,而是会涉及时间的一些简单的加减运算。要注意一些关键词,如: a quarter(to/past), half (past), daily, weekly, fortnight 等。

2. 商品的价格。同样,在短对话中,该类试题也涉及一些简单的加减乘除运算。要注意一些关键词,如:10% off, discount, double, half the price, couple, pair, dozen, a real bargain, on

sale, change 等。尤其要注意单件商品的价格,买多件商品是否优惠、找零以及最后的问题是说话人要付的钱、单件商品的价格,还是买若干商品需要付的钱。

【答题技巧】

速记信息。这类题目的对话中一般都不会只出现一个数字,所以要对数字及相关要点信息进行速记。

听清问题。做这类题目时,必须清楚地抓住问题是针对什么提出,然后才能根据记录的信息将答案对号入座。

不要直取答案。这类题目的答案一般都不会是原文中数字信息的再现,往往需要经过简单的运算才能得出答案。

【典型例题】

【例3】　　A) $ 8.60.　　B) $ 4.30.　　C) $ 6.40.　　D) $ 1.40.

W: Here's a ten-dollar bill. Give me two tickets for tonight's show, please.

M: Sure. Two tickets and here's a dollar forty cents in change.

Q: How much does one ticket cost?

【解析】在听对话的过程中需要对听到的几个数字进行速记:ten-dollar bill, two tickets, a dollar forty cents' change,通过对这几个数字的运算可以得到试题的正确答案B)。

Part IV　Applied Writing

Résumé（简历）

简历就是对个人学历、经历、特长、爱好及其他有关情况所做的简明扼要的书面介绍。简历是个人形象,包括资历与能力的书面表述,对于求职者而言,是必不可少的一种应用文。参加求职面试时,简历既能为介绍自己提供思路和基本素材,又能供主持面试者详细阅读。面试之后,还可以供对方存入计算机或归档备查。

Sample 1

Résumé
Sandy Bright

2066 HONGAN BUILDING
NO. 233 JINTAI ROAD, BEIJING
PHONE: 13912345678
EMAIL: shen16900@sina.com

OBJECTIVE

A position that will further develop my strong marketing skills, and a training and

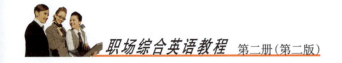

counseling position with a business firm.

EXPERIENCE

Overseas Marketing Manager, PHE LO ADD Ltd., Singapore, 1999—present

Marketing Manager, G.S. STONE Ltd., Singapore, 1993—1999

Assistant Manager, Sony Music Co., Malaysia, 1988—1993

EDUCATION

Master of Business Administration, Boston University, 1990

Bachelor of Arts, Vocational Counseling, Virginia, Commonwealth University, Richmond, Virginia, 1982

COMPUTER OPERATING SKILLS

Macintosh; PageMaker, Word; WordPerfect, Excel and PowerPoint.

PERSONAL

Enjoy challenges and working with people.

Interested in increasing productivity.

Sample 2

Résumé
Sandy Bright
65 Jones Rd EARLVILLE NSW 4444   0488 888 888(m)
j.sample@example.com

CAREER OBJECTIVE

    A position with an innovative, results-oriented firm where my excellent numerical, analytical and strategic thinking skills will be valued.

EDUCATION

1999—2001	Bachelor of Commerce Major in Accounting
	University of New South Wales
1998	Higher School Certificate

EMPLOYMENT

2000—2001	Accounts Assistant—Summer Vacation
	Bib and Bob Accountants
1999—2000	Sales Assistant—Part Time
	Value Supermarkets

KEY SKILL

    Communication; Teamwork; Numeracy

INTERESTS

    Soccer; Chess; Sculpture

REFERENCES	
Professor Wu Sha	
Head of School of Accounting	Manager Woolworths
University of New South Wales	Earlville Store

(contact details available on request)

Assignment: *Suppose you are Alice Wang. You would like to apply for the position of sales manager of ABC Company. Please write a résumé for it.*

Part V   Cultural Express

Job Hunting Tips

Network!

Think of the people you know—relatives, friends, professors, classmates, co-workers at summer jobs, and others. Make more of an effort to meet with people, and use these conversations to ask their advice, to make them aware of your job search, to learn more about their jobs or their organizations, and to get the names of others who might be useful in your job search.

Target your resume.

Make sure your résumé is targeted to the employers who receive it. Make sure your résumé is easy to read and the most important details stand out. Make more than one résumé if you are applying to more than one industry.

Be prepared.

You should have a copy of your résumé with you at all times. It is also a good idea to have fresh copies of your résumé prepared in case you are called to an interview at the last minute.

Create a contact database.

Write down all the employers you contact, the date you sent your résumé, any contact made, people you talk to, and notes about those contacts. Keep a notepad with you at all times—take notes as soon as you hear about an opportunity or when you leave an interview. Get into the habit of updating your database daily.

Make a "to do" list every day.

This will help you organize your list of priorities and keep you focused on finding that perfect job.

Try the buddy system.

Link up with a friend who is also job hunting. Arrange to speak weekly and report on accomplishments, best practices, and future plans.

Learn how to talk about yourself.

Throughout your job search, you will speak with many people at different levels. You must be comfortable having conversations about yourself with other people. Keep in mind that you never know who may end up being useful to your job hunt.

Prepare an elevator speech.

You never know who you'll meet in an elevator, in line at the coffee shop, or on the street. Know what your skills are and how to communicate them. You should be able to tell prospective employers and others you meet what you can offer. You should also be able to talk about how your skills relate to the industries that interest you.

Find out all there is to know about employers in your field.

Remain current on any issues or developments in the field, read trade journals or professional publications, and read the newspaper. It is extremely impressive during an interview if you know about the latest merger or takeover in the industry.

Practice for each interview.

Preparation is key to interviewing well. Friends, relatives, and career services counselors can help you formulate strong answers to questions you might not anticipate. Look at the list of possible questions on the interviewing section and prepare yourself.

Follow up with leads immediately.

If you find out about a position late in the day, call right then. Don't wait until the next day.

Stay confident.

Job hunting takes time and energy. Remain confident, but prepare yourself for challenges ahead. Don't get disgruntled if you are still looking for a job and it seems like everyone you know has an offer. Most students find their jobs after graduation.

拓展词汇

书面申请材料

résumé 简历；CV(curriculum vitae) 简历；school transcript 成绩单；reference 推荐；a letter of recommendation 推荐信；referee 推荐人；certificate 证书；diploma 学位证书；graduate certificate 毕业证书

工作

employment 工作；work experience 工作经验；work history 工作经历；entry-level work 初级工作；previous work 以前的工作；position 职位；job title 职位；secondary occupation 第二职业；promotion 提升

Unit 1　Job Hunting

工作要求

responsibility 职责；duty 职责；able to meet deadline 有能力在限期内完成工作；work under pressure 在压力下工作；pay attention to detail 细心；good cooperation skills 良好的合作能力；oral and written skills 口头和笔头技能；teamwork ability 团队工作能力；communication skills 交流能力

面试常见问题

Tell us about yourself? 介绍一下你自己。
Tell me about your family or your girlfriend /boyfriend?
说说你的家庭或者你的女朋友/男朋友。
How do your friends describe you?
你的朋友如何描述你？
Why would you leave you last job and join our company?
为什么离开原来的公司而加入我们公司？
Why have you applied for this job?
你申请这份工作的理由是什么？
What is your understanding of the company?
你对本公司有哪些了解？
Why should we hire you?
我们为什么要雇用你？
Why are you the best person for this job?
你为什么是这份工作最佳人选？
What are your strengths and weaknesses?
你的强项和不足是什么？
Where do you see yourself in 5 years?
五年后的你将是什么样子？
What do you pride most in your life?
你生活中最引以为豪的事情是什么？
What's your biggest failure in your life?
你生活中最大的失败是什么？
How do you handle your conflict with your colleagues at work?
你如何处理和同事之间的冲突？
How do you work under pressure /stress?
你如何在压力下工作？

21

Unit 2

Interesting Jobs

Learning Objectives:

You are able to:
- ☞ Comment on different jobs
- ☞ Write a business contract

You are suggested to:
- ☞ Recognize the English expressions of different jobs
- ☞ Be familiar with some famous corporations

• Unit 2 Interesting Jobs •

Part I Listening and Speaking

Warm-up

Task 1

Directions: Can you tell what they do for a living? Please describe the people in the pictures.

| nurse | farmer | architect | teacher |
| photographer | worker | doctor | lawyer |

(1) (2) (3) (4)

(5) (6) (7) (8)

Task 2

Directions: Work with your partner and match the following Chinese phrases with their English equivalents.

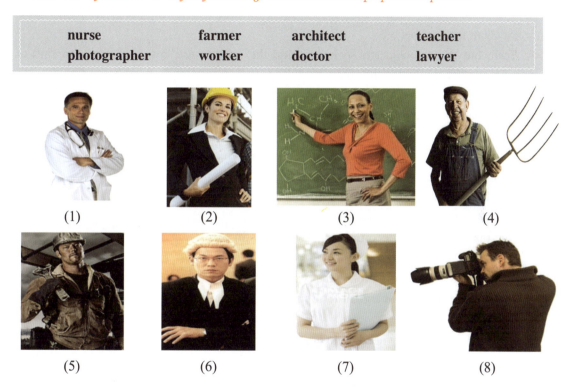

采购经理 ☆
首席执行官/总经理 ☆
仓库管理员 ☆
市场/营销主管 ☆
市场分析/调研人员 ☆
外贸/贸易经理/主管 ☆
财务/会计助理 ☆
报关员 ☆

★ CEO/GM/President
★ Marketing Supervisor
★ Market Analyst/ Research Analyst
★ Purchasing Manager
★ Warehouse Specialist
★ Trading Manager/Supervisor
★ Customs Specialist
★ Finance/Accounting Assistant

23

Oral Practice

Task 1

Directions: Read the dialogue and answer the following questions.

Talking About Career Choice

M: Have you thought about what you want to do, Betty?

W: Oh, yeah, Jack. I've been looking for jobs, I really want to start interviewing soon.

M: I've heard there're some good jobs in the government. They are pretty secure and offer excellent medical benefits.

W: Yeah, but those jobs seem so boring and the salaries are low. I'd prefer to find an interesting company to work for.

M: Well, what about something like sales work? You could be independent, creative...

W: Well, yeah, I really like the idea. I bet I could meet lots of different people and...

M: Sure!

W: ... do some traveling and maybe get out of the office...

M: Yeah, sounds nice! I wonder how much money you can make in sales, though.

W: Mm, I don't know... But, actually, I think I'd rather be on commission...

M: Really?

W: ... so that I'd get paid according to how successful I am.

M: Yes?

W: I could make much more money that way. I think I'd prefer that to getting a salary.

M: Well, I think you've got a great future in sales.

1. What would Betty really need to do before she gets a job?
   □ To have an interview.   □ To get help from Jack.
2. What job does Jack suggest?
   □ Sales work.   □ Jobs in the government.
3. What job does Betty prefer?
   □ Sales work.   □ Jobs in the government.
4. What salary does Betty expect to get?
   □ Salary based on commission.   □ Salary only.

• Unit 2 Interesting Jobs •

Task 2

Directions: Suppose you are the manager of the Personnel Department of ABC Company. Your partner is a new employee. Here is a table of positions. Please introduce the different departments and staff in your company to the new employee and role-play a conversation with your partner. Then reverse roles and do it again.

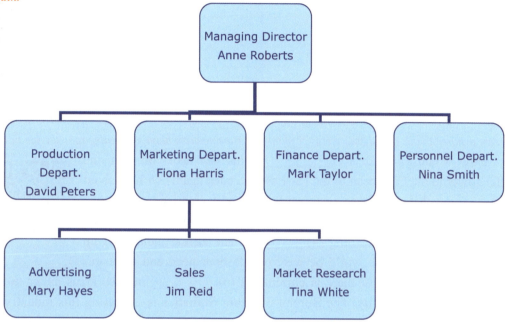

Listening Practice

Task 1

Directions: Listen to the dialogue, and tick (√) in the box at the end of the correct answer.

1. What job does Susan apply for?
   A. The job of a sales representative. ☐
   B. The job of a sales manager. ☐
   C. The job of a company representative. ☐
2. How many years of work experience does Susan have?
   A. One year. ☐
   B. Two years. ☐
   C. Three years. ☐
3. Does Susan have to work on Saturdays?
   A. Yes, she does. ☐
   B. No, she doesn't. ☐
   C. It is not mentioned. ☐

4. How long will the training last?
   A. Two weeks. ☐
   B. Three weeks.. ☐
   C. Four weeks. ☐
5. When will Susan know the result of the job interview?
   A. In about one week. ☐
   B. In about two weeks. ☐
   C. In about three weeks. ☐

Task 2

Directions: In this section you will hear a recorded short passage. The passage will be read three times. You are required to put the missing words or phrases in the numbered blanks according to what you hear.

How would you like a (1) _____ that can take you from the Eiffel Tower to the Caribbean to the Far East and back again? Or how about a (2) _____ that grants free air travel to you and your friends or family? Working in the (3) _____ industry can give you all this in what many find to be a fun and rewarding (4) _____ . The airline industry is an important one around the world because people both need and want to (5) _____ . In some areas of airline jobs, there is currently a (6) _____ in such areas as air traffic control and airport security. The Bureau of Labor Statistics is expecting this industry to (7) _____ considerably in the next few years as the (8) _____ gets better and more people are willing to travel. If you are willing to work while you are having fun, there are also (9) _____ for advancement in most aviation industry jobs, as well as the possibility of being transferred to other (10) _____ .

Task 3

Directions: Listen to the conversation and work in pairs to decide whether the following statements are true or false according to what you have heard. Write "T" if the statement is true and "F" if it is false.

_____ 1. The last job Alice introduced to Frank was fairly good.
_____ 2. Alice thinks Frank is qualified for this job.
_____ 3. The company pays a basic salary and a high bonus.
_____ 4. The company wants college graduates with two years marketing experience.
_____ 5. Frank is not interested in the job at all.

• Unit 2　Interesting Jobs •

Part II　Reading

Text A

Before Reading:

1. Are you familiar with the following pictures?
2. Do you know what should be prepared before the wedding?

Event Planning: Wedding

Event planning is a relatively new career field. There are now courses that help people who are trying to break into the field. There must be training for an event planner to handle all the pressure and work efficiently. This career deals with a lot of communication and organization aspects. There are many different names for an event planner such as a conference coordinator, a special event coordinator, and a meeting manager.

Event planners' work is considered either stressful or energizing. This line of work is also considered fast-paced and demanding. Planners face deadlines and communicating with many people at one time. Planners spend most of their time in offices, but when meeting with clients the work is usually on-site at the location where the event is taking place. Some physical activity is required such as carrying boxes of materials and decorations or supplies needed for the event. Also, long working hours can be a part of the job. The day the event is taking place could start as early as

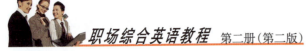

5:00 a.m., and then the planner may work until midnight. Working on weekends is sometimes required, which is when many events take place.

Weddings are significant events in people's lives and therefore, couples are often willing to spend considerable sums of money to ensure their wedding is organized as perfectly as possible. A wedding planner is a professional who assists with the design, planning and management of a client's wedding. Professional wedding planners exist throughout the world, most notably in the USA, UK and Western Europe. There are various wedding planning courses available to those who wish to pursue the career.

Wedding planners are often used by couples who work long hours and have little spare time available for sourcing and managing wedding venues and wedding suppliers. Planners are also popular with couples planning a destination wedding, where the documentation and paperwork can be complicated. Any country where a wedding is held requires different procedures depending on the nationality of the bride and the groom.

The services of a wedding planner can include:

- Interviewing the couple and the parents to identify their needs;

- Budget preparation;
- Planning a detailed checklist (from about a year in advance to a few days after the wedding);
- Guest list preparation;
- Arrangement of event venues (hotels, churches, etc.);
- Identifying and hiring of wedding professionals and service providers (caterers, photographers, beautician, florists, bakers, etc.), and preparation and execution of contracts;
- Coordination of deliveries and services on the wedding day;
- Have a back-up plan in the event of a disaster;
- Assist and prepare legal documentation and translations—especially for destination weddings.

Unit 2　Interesting Jobs

New Words

(标★为A级词汇，标☆为超纲词汇)

coordinator	/kəʊˈɔːdɪneɪtə/	n.	协调者；同等的人(或物)
stressful	/ˈstresfʊl, -f(ə)l/	adj.	有压力的
fast-paced		adj.	快步调的，快节奏的
deadline	/ˈdedlaɪn/	n.	最后期限；截止期限；死线；原稿截止时间
decoration	/dekəˈreɪʃ(ə)n/	n.	装饰，装潢；装饰品；装饰图案，装饰风格；奖章
considerable	/kənˈsɪd(ə)rəb(ə)l/	adj.	相当大（或多）的；该注意的，应考虑的
★professional	/prəˈfeʃ(ə)n(ə)l/	n.	专业人士
		adj.	职业的，专业的
venue	/ˈvenjuː/	n.	犯罪地点，案发地点；会场；(尤指)体育比赛场所
documentation	/ˌdɒkjʊmenˈteɪʃ(ə)n/	n.	证明某事属实的证据；记录；参考资料；文献的编集，文件分类
nationality	/næʃəˈnælətɪ/	n.	国籍；国家
checklist	/ˈtʃeklɪst/	n.	清单；检查表；备忘录；目录册
caterer	/ˈkeɪtərə/	n.	(尤指职业的)酒席承办人，提供饮食及服务的人；筹办者
beautician	/bjuːˈtɪʃ(ə)n/	n.	美容师
florist	/ˈflɒrɪst/	n.	花商，花农，花卉研究者
baker	/ˈbeɪkə/	n.	面包师；烤炉
★execution	/ˌeksɪˈkjuːʃ(ə)n/	n.	实行，履行，执行，贯彻；做成，完成
contract	/ˈkɒntrækt/	n.	契约；婚约；[法]契约法；行贿
★delivery	/dɪˈlɪv(ə)rɪ/	n.	传送，投递
back-up			备份

Phrases and Expressions

Event Planning	（婚礼）事务策划

Exercises

I. Reading Comprehension

Directions: Circle the right answer for the following questions.

1. Which one is not true about event planning?
   A. It needs a lot of communication and organization.
   B. It is a career field which has developed for a long time.
   C. The people who work on it must be trained to handle all the work.
   D. The people who work on it can be called an event coordinator.
2. What is an event planner?
   A. They almost stay in offices to handle all the work.
   B. They have to work on weekends.
   C. Their work needs communication with many people.
   D. Their work is an easy job without pressure.
3. Which one is true about wedding planning?
   A. It often exists in some developed countries, like USA, UK.
   B. It refers to the organization and management of a wedding.
   C. It is very helpful for the couples who have lots of spare time.
   D. It has one course to train people who want to work on it.
4. The right time for planning detailed checklist should begin from_____.
   A. a few days before wedding   B. a few years before wedding
   C. one month before wedding   D. one year before wedding
5. Which is not the service provided in a wedding?
   A. Photographing.   B. Delivery.   C. Baking.   D. Washing.

II. True or False

Directions: Decide whether the following statements are true or false according to the text. Write "T" if the statement is true and "F" if it is false.

_____ 1. Event planners should finish their work before a certain time.
_____ 2. Event planners don't need to do some physical activities.
_____ 3. The guest list is prepared by the couples and the parents.
_____ 4. It is necessary to prepare two plans for the wedding event.
_____ 5. There is no document and paperwork for a wedding planning.

III. Word Usage

Directions: Complete each of the following sentences with the correct form of the italicized word given in the brackets.

1. She's very good at coping with _____ *(stress)* situations.

2. He made a successful _____ (career) in business.
3. Everything has two contradictory _____ (aspect).
4. I'm very _____ (organize) and extremely capable.
5. These snakes can be _____ (identify) readily.
6. _____ (prepare) for the wedding takes very much time and money.
7. No _____ (profession) participated in the contest.
8. What _____ (course) have you completed?

IV. Blank Filling

Directions: Translate the Chinese part of the following sentences with the correct form of the words and expressions in the box.

coordinate	decoration	deadline	professional
documentation	delivery	venue	client

1. I hope we can finish this work before the _____. (最后期限)
2. Finally, ensure that you bring the required _____ with you. (文件)
3. She picked a large bunch of flowers for table _____. (装饰)
4. You must _____ what you said with what you did. (与……一致)
5. Could you update us on the date, _____ and agenda items? (地点)
6. She can't come to the telephone; she's serving a _____. (顾客)
7. I need a _____ to sort out my finances. (专业人士)
8. The strike caused a great delay in the _____ of the mail. (投递)

V. Translation

Directions: Put the following English sentences into Chinese.

1. Couples who are very busy sometimes hire a wedding planner to help them with their preparations.
2. Budget cutbacks forced the company to let go of several employees.
3. They celebrate their wedding anniversary annually.
4. Emphasis on teamwork, good communication and coordination ability and organizational capacity.
5. A big wedding needs special clothing, flowers, food preparation, photographs and music.

Text B

Before Reading:

1. What is your image of "Mr. Right" or "Miss Right"?
2. What do you think is important in a successful marriage?

Premarital Counseling

What is premarital counseling and is it worth the time and money? It has been well documented that since the mid 1980s, 50 % of all marriages in the US result in divorce. Interestingly, it is the seventh year of marriage which presents itself as the most popular time to say goodbye. The latter statistic most likely gave rise to the saying we all know these days as "the seven year itch".

After hearing these statistics, one cannot help but wonder, what does keep a couple together? What commonalities do successful marriages share? Research has proven that certain qualities will produce a successful marriage, including: high income level, compatibility, communication and conflict resolution skills as well as religious involvement. Evidence of the most common contributing factors to divorce include: marrying at a young age, poverty, and a low education level.

Truth be told, marriage is not only a beautiful love fest but also a living breathing partnership. There is love to grow, bills to pay, children to rear, dinners to prepare, a home to maintain, diapers to change, lunches to be made, social responsibilities to attend to... and on and on. A well-established partnership is required to successfully manage the family.

A lot of married couples admit that the real stresses arrive after the first child is born. Anyone that has kids is well aware of how un-sexy a new parent will feel at the end of the day. Premarital counseling offers the opportunity for a couple to discuss changes and stressful moments that may surface throughout a marriage. In premarital counseling, couples discuss topics such as child rearing, finances, life goals and work out any issues that may surface as a result of different philosophies. Premarital counseling allows a couple to start the marriage off, communicating about conflict and feelings.

While premarital counseling may be a growing trend for couples in the 21st century, it is commonplace for Catholics to undergo a form of premarital counseling before marriage. Pre-Cana is the course all Catholic couples must undergo before they can be married in a Catholic church. Research has revealed that Catholics have the lowest divorce rate, whether or not this fact is a result of mandatory Pre-Cana is to be determined.

One could argue successfully that what ultimately keeps a couple together is questionable and reliant on many determining factors. However, premarital counseling will offer a couple opportunities that will better prepare them for challenges before them. As mentioned above, a couple has a 50/50 chance of remaining married throughout their lives. With odds like those, opting for premarital counseling makes a lot of sense.

• Unit 2 Interesting Jobs •

New Words

（标★为A级词汇,标☆为超纲词汇）

☆premarital	/priːˈmærɪt(ə)l/	n.	婚前
★counseling	/ˈkaʊns(ə)lɪŋ/	n.	咨询
document	/ˈdɒkjʊm(ə)nt/	n.	文件
		v.	记载（详情）；用文件证明（或证实）
divorce	/dɪˈvɔːs/	n.	离婚
★statistic	/stəˈtɪstɪk/	n.	统计数字；统计资料
★compatibility	/kəmˌpætɪˈbɪlətɪ/	n.	适合
rear	/rɪə/	v.	养育
Catholic	/ˈkæθ(ə)lɪk/	n.	天主教徒
mandatory	/ˈmændət(ə)rɪ/	adj.	强制的；命令的；义务的

Phrases and Expressions

| premarital counseling | 婚前咨询 |
| the seven year itch | 七年之痒 |

Exercises

I. Summary

Directions: Fill in the blanks with the appropriate words according to your understanding.

Premarital counseling is a very useful way to reduce the risk of (1)_____. It is researched that a good (2)_____ is a well established (3)_____ of the couples. The real pressures and (4)_____ in daily life will bring some problems to the couples. Premarital counseling can help couples to (5)_____ changes and stressful moments. It is proactive in that it (6)_____ forming negative relationship habits. (7)_____ are common to have a form of premarital counseling (8)_____ marriage and they have the lowest divorce (9)_____. Generally speaking, premarital counseling is a good method for couples to prepare for (10)_____ in their marriage.

II. Reading Comprehension

Directions: Circle the right answer for the following questions.

1. Which statement is true?

    A. It is documented that the US had a high divorce rate since 1980s.

    B. Most of the couples get divorced in their seventh year.

    C. Premarital counseling can reduce the risk of divorce.

    D. There are lots of trifles in real life after the wedding.

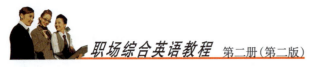

2. The qualities which produce a good marriage do not conclude _____.
   A. compatibility   B. high income   C. young age   D. communication
3. Which is not the stressful moment in real life?
   A. Pay the bills.   B. Prepare the meals.   C. Earn more money.   D. Play with the babies.
4. Premarital counseling can help couples _____.
   A. rear their children   B. solve financial problems
   C. communicate feelings   D. form positive habits
5. What is Pre-Cana?
   A. It is used to reduce the divorce rate of all couples.
   B. It is a form of premarital counseling for Catholics.
   C. It is a course for all couples undergoing before marriage.
   D. It is the only reason that Catholics have the lowest divorce rate.

III. Vocabulary & Structures

Directions: Fill in the blanks with the proper words or expressions in the box.

counsel	statistics	divorce	undergo
mandatory	odd	opt	questionable

1. Couples may agree to _____ each other after a separation.
2. The explorers had to _____ much suffering.
3. Their motives for undertaking this study are highly _____.
4. She looks a bit _____. I wonder what has happened to her.
5. Attendance is _____ at all meetings.
6. They _____ for more holiday instead of more pay.
7. _____ suggest(s) that the population of this country will be double in ten years' time.
8. He refused to listen to the old man's _____ .

IV. Translation

Directions: Put the following English sentences into Chinese.

1. Don't rush into marriage; you might regret it later.
2. A happy home life needs the efforts from both sides of the couple.
3. Recently a lot of couples have been attending marriage counseling.
4. Communication, of course, doesn't need to be in words.
5. My duty to my family lies before my own interests.

Part III Strategies

词汇解析

词汇部分历来是考试的一个重点,这部分共20题,分为10道单项选择题和10道选词填空题两个部分。

一、解释参照法:利用句中的释义推导

此种方法的依据是词是对另一部分词汇意思的解释。

1. The medicine is for sale everywhere. You can get it at _____ chemist's.
   A) each   B) some   C) certain   D) any

   正确选项为D)。本题中前一句中的everywhere就决定了第二句中的空格处填(at) any (chemist's)。

2. The manager spoke highly of _____ such as loyalty, courage and truthfulness shown by his employees.
   A) virtues   B) features   C) properties   D) characteristics

   正确选项为A)。本句中as后面的名词loyalty(忠诚),courage(勇气) and truthfulness (实事求是)是对空格处名词进行的解释。本句中的三个名词归纳起来都属于人应当具有的 "美德",所以本题的答案为A)。

3. I hope that you'll be more careful in typing the letter. Don't _____ anything.
   A) lack   B) withdraw   C) omit   D) leak

   正确选项为C)。前边的I hope that you'll be more careful决定的后边的要填C)项omit, 意思是"遗漏"。

二、因果参照法:利用句中的因果关系推导

这种方法的依据是题干中的分句之间存在的因果关系。

1. Some old people don't like pop songs because they can't _____ so much noise.
   A) resist   B) sustain   C) tolerate   D) undergo

   正确选项为C)。本句从don't like…,推出后面的can't tolerate,表示"不能容忍"的意思。

2. The poetry of Ezra Pound is sometimes difficult to understand because it contains so many _____ references.
   A) obscure   B) acute   C) notable   D) objective

   正确选项为A)。通过结果"difficult to understand"推出正确项"obscure",意思是"含糊难解的"。其他三个选项的意思分别是:B)敏锐,剧烈的;C)显著的,明显的;D)客观的。

3. Being somewhat short sighted, she had the habit of _____ at people.

　　A) glancing　　　B) peering　　　C) staring　　　D) scanning

正确选项为 C)。通过原因"short sighted"推出正确选项 C) staring,意思是"凝视,盯着"。

4. Since the matter was extremely _____, we dealt with it immediately.

　　A) tough　　　B) tense　　　C) urgent　　　D) instant

正确选项为 C)。后半句中的副词"immediately"可以推出前半句的"urgent"(迫切的,紧急的)。

5. The shy girl felt _____ and uncomfortable when she could not answer her teacher's questions.

　　A) amazed　　　B) awkward　　　C) curious　　　D) amused

正确选项为 B)。句中 and 后边的 uncomfortable 是空白处所填入词的近义词,所给四个选项中只有 awkward(尴尬的,难堪的)与 uncomfortable 意思相近。

三、转折参照法:利用句中的转折关系推导

这种方法的依据是题干中存在的转折关系。做题时可以通过转折词来确定选项,也可以通过句中词来确定选项中的转折词。

1. Even though he was guilty, the _____ judge did not send him to prison.

　　A) merciful　　　B) impartial　　　C) conscientious　　　D) conspicuous

正确选项为 A)。有罪而没有被判刑,表明法官是一个"仁慈"的人。所以 A)项正确。其他三项的意思分别是:B)正直的、公正的;C)有良心的;D)显著的。

2. _____ their differences, the couple were developing an obvious and genuine affection for each other.

　　A) But for　　　B) For all　　　C) Above all　　　D) Except for

正确选项为 B)。句中的 their differences, obvious and genuine affection 可确定选项中的转折词只能是 for all,意思是"尽管"。

3. Most nurses are women but in the higher ranks of the medical profession women are in a _____.

　　A) scarcity　　　B) minority　　　C) minimum　　　D) shortage

正确选项为 B)。通过 most...but... 可确定本题的正确选项为 B),与 most 相对,表达"少数"的意思。

四、对比比较参照法：利用句中的反义或对比推导

此种方法是通过句中的转折词、反义词或对比词来确定选项。

1. These goods are _____ for export, though a few of them may be sold on the home market.

　　A) essentially　　　B) completely　　　C) necessarily　　　D) remarkably

正确选项为A)。通过转折词though和对比词export与home market以及a few可确定选项为A)，意思是"基本上"。其他三项都不符合句意。

2. Mr. Morgan can be very sad _____, though in public he is extremely cheerful.

　　A) by himself　　　B) in person　　　C) in private　　　D) as individual

正确选项为C)。通过后半句的转折词though和对比词in public...cheerful来确定sad in private，意思是"私下里"。

3. Why should anyone want to read _____ of books by great authors when the real pleasure comes from reading the originals?

　　A) themes　　　B) insights　　　C) digests　　　D) leaflets

正确选项为C)。这里originals(原著)与空格处的词相对，所以空格处的词意思应当是"文摘，摘录"，显然，只有C)项为正确选择。

4. I think she hurt my feelings _____ rather than by accident as she claimed.

　　A) virtually　　　B) deliberately　　　C) literally　　　D) appropriately

正确选项为B)。rather than表明了by accident与空格处意思相对。by accident的意思是"偶然地，不经意地"，与此相对的应当是deliberately，"故意地"。

五、语意环境参照法：利用句中的语意环境推导

这里指的是纯粹根据题干的上下文来确定选项，也就是说选项的意义来确定正确选项。

1. The new appointment of our president _____ from the very beginning of next semester.

　　A) takes effect　　　B) takes part　　　C) takes place　　　D) takes turns

正确选项为A)。四个选项的意思分别为：A)生效；B)参加；C)发生；D)轮流。从本句句意来看，只有A)项符合句意，本句大意是：对新校长的任命从下学期伊始生效。

2. Finding a job in such a big company has always been _____ his wildest dreams.

　　A) under　　　B) over　　　C) above　　　D) beyond

正确选项为D)。一般来说能在一个大公司里谋到一份差事很不容易，所以她"超出了"一般人的梦想，所以只能选D) beyond，表示"超出……之外"的意思。

六、利用动词词组中的介词或副词确定正确选项

命题人员想考查考生是否掌握了某一动词词组的用法，在设计四个选项时，有时会让一个动词出现在四个选项中，只是后边的介词或副词不一样。在做这一类题时，如果我们认识某一词组，根据自己的判断毫不犹豫地选择你认为是正确的选项。如果不认识或拿不准它们的意义，我们可以根据上下文并以动词后边的介词或副词进行推导，如下例：

1. Having decided to rent a flat, we _____ contacting all the accommodation agencies in the city.

   A) set about   B) set down   C) set out   D) set up

   本题的答案为A）。本句前边说"已经决定租房，我们联系房屋中介商……"这里需要填"开始"的意思。从动词后的四个介词来说，只有about有表示"将来"（be about）的意思，所以A）为正确答案。需顺便补充的是，set about这一结构中，about是介词，需要用动词的-ing形式。

2. One day I _____ a newspaper article about the retirement of an English professor at a nearby state college.

   A) came across   B) came about   C) came after   D) came at

   本题的答案为A）。由于文中有"One day"这一时间状语和下文的意思，如果大家知道come across表示"（意外）碰到"，那就毫不犹豫地选A）。但如果不知道come across有此意义，我们根据四个介词的基本意义也可以判断A）为正确答案（across交叉、穿过，come across 碰巧读到）。

3. When he realized the police had spotted him, the man _____ the exit as quickly as possible.

   A) made off   B) made for   C) made out   D) made up

   本题的答案为B）。这里空格处要填的是表示"走向"之意，这里只有"for"表示在同一水平线上"向……方向"。注意，句中有exit一词，表示the man是在一个建筑物内，所以不可能用out the exit（注意上下文），而且out是一个副词，后面接名词时需要有介词of，所以正确选项是B）而不是C）。

七、利用动词词组中的动词确定选项

有些题的四个选项中的介词或副词一样，而动词则不一样，这时我们就可以利用动词的区别来确定正确选项，如下例：

If you _____ the bottle and cigarettes, you'll be much healthier.

A) take off   B) keep off   C) get off   D) set off

本题答案为B）。keep与off合在一起是"与……保持距离，远离……"的意思，根据句子的意思"如果你不喝酒（这里bottle是替代，以名词bottle代动词喝酒）、不吸烟，你就会更健康"，正确选项为B）。

八、利用句中的语法结构与固定搭配推导

1. It is useful to be able to predict _____ the extent which a price change will affect supply and demand.

   A) from   B) with   C) to   D) for

   正确选项是C）。to the extent是固定搭配，which引导的定语从句修饰先行词extent，所以空格处应填入的介词为to.

2. You cannot be _____ careful when you drive a car.

　　A) very　　　　　B) so　　　　　　C) too　　　　　　D) enough

正确选项为C)。cannot...too是固定搭配，表示"再……也不为过，越……越好"的意思。

九、根据词的同现确定正确选择项

同现指同一些词有时会出现在同一个语义场中，即同时出现在一个句子中，这就成了我们答题的依据。

1. Remember that customers don't _____ about prices in that city.

　　A) debate　　　　B) consult　　　　C) dispute　　　　D) bargain

正确选项是D)。空格后的名词price决定其前的动词用bargain，构成bargain about，意思是"就……讨价还价"。

2. A _____ to this problem is expected to be found before long.

　　A) result　　　　B) response　　　C) settlement　　　D) solution

正确选项是D)。只有solution"措施"才能和problem同时出现，表示"某一问题的解决措施"。

3. Over a third of the population was estimated to have no _____ to the health service.

　　A) assessment　　B) assignment　　C) exception　　　D) access

正确选项为D)。"have/gain access to"这一词组的意思是"有使用……的权利"。其他三项均不能和have...to同时使用。

十、利用固定词组推导

这里包括两种，一种是四个选项本身就是固定词组，另一种情况是句中的前面或后面的词与选项构成固定词组。

1. The politician says he will _____ the welfare of the people.

　　A) prey on　　　　B) take on　　　　C) get at　　　　　D) see to

正确选项是D)。所给四个选项意思分别是：A)捕食，掠夺；B)从事，担任；C)到达，得到；D)注意，照料。可见只有D)项才符合题意。

2. When I said goodbye to her, she _____ the door.

　　A) saw me at　　　B) set me off　　C) sent me to　　　D) showed me to

正确选项是D)。show sb. to the door意思是"把某人送到门口"，其他三项均不符合习惯表达法。

3. The car _____ halfway for no reason.

　　A) broke off　　　B) broke down　　C) broke up　　　　D) broke out

正确选项是B)。broke down的意思是"抛锚，出故障"，其他三项不符合题意。

4. The political future of the president is now hanging by a _____.

　　A) thread　　　　B) cord　　　　　C) string　　　　　D) rope

正确选项为A)。hang by a thread是固定用法，意思是"千钧一发，处境危险"。

十一、根据常识选答案

有些试题表述的是一个常识性知识,只要我们了解该常识,问题就迎刃而解。

1. A person's calorie requirements vary _____ his life.

    A) across   B) throughout   C) over   D) within

此题正确选项应为B)。本题描述的常识是:在人的生命过程中对热量的需求是不断变化的。

2. Floods cause billions of dollars worth of property damage _____ .

    A) relatively   B) actually   C) annually   D) comparatively

正确选项为C)。从句意来看,空白处需要填入的应是一个表示时间的词,所给四个选项中只有C)项annually表示"每年"的意思。其他三项A)相对地;B)实际上;D)相比较而言,都不符合题意。

Part IV Applied Writing

Contract(合同)

合同是当事人或当事双方之间设立、变更、终止民事关系的协议。涉外商务合同按繁简不同,可以采取不同的书面形式,如正式合同(Contract)、协议书(Agreement)、确认书(Confirmation)、备忘录(Memorandum)、订单(Order)等。一份正式的合同通常由以下几个部分组成:

一、合同名称(Title)

二、前文(Preamble)

一般包括订约日期和地点(Date and Place of Signing),合同当事人及其国籍、主要营业场所或住所(Signing Parties and Their Nationalities, Principal Place of Business or Residence Addresses),当事人合法依据(Each Party's Authority,如该公司是"按当地法律正式组织而存在的"/ A Corporation Duly Organized and Existing Under the Laws of XXX),订约缘由/说明条款(Recitals or Whereas Clause)。

三、正文(Body)

一般包括定义条款、基本条款和一般条款。

定义条款(Definition Clause):对合同中重复出现的关键名词术语进行明确定义,给出明确解释。

四、结尾条款(Witness Clause)

一般包括份数、使用的文字和效力(Concluding Sentence)、签名(Signature)。

Sample 1

1. NAME OF COMMODITY AND SCOPE OF THE CONTRACT
2. PRICE
3. PAYMENT
4. PACKING

    IN WITNESS WHEREOF, this contract has been executed effective as of the date first above written.

THE BUYER	THE SELLER
ABC Company	China Yunhai Tea Export Company
By: Tom Smith	By: Wang Fang
Date: 7/12/12	Date: 7/12/12

Sample 2

Sales Contract

The undersigned Seller and Buyer have agreed to close the following transactions according to the terms and conditions set forth as below:

1. Name, Specifications and Quality of Commodity:
2. Quantity:
3. Unit Price and Terms of Delivery:

The terms FOB, CFR, or CIF shall be subject to the International Rules for the Interpretation of Trade Terms (INCOTERMS 2000) provided by International Chamber of Commerce (ICC) unless otherwise stipulated herein.

4. Total Amount:
5. More or Less:_____‰.
6. Time of Shipment:

Within _____ days after receipt of L/C allowing transhipment and partial shipment.

7. Terms of Payment:

By Confirmed, Irrevocable, Transferable and Divisible L/C (letter of credit) to be available by sight draft to reach the Seller before _____ and to remain valid for negotiation in China until _____ after the Time of Shipment. The L/C must specify that transshipment and partial shipments are allowed.

The Buyer shall establish a Letter of Credit before the above-stipulated time, failing which, the Seller shall have the right to rescind this Contract upon the arrival of the notice at Buyer or to accept whole or part of this Contract non fulfilled by the Buyer, or to lodge a claim for the direct losses sustained, if any.

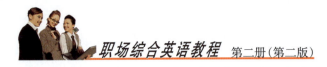

8. Packing:

9. Insurance:

Covering _____ Risks for _____ 110% of Invoice Value to be effected by the _____.

10. Quality/Quantity discrepancy:

In case of quality discrepancy, claim should be filed by the Buyer within 30 days after the arrival of the goods at port of destination, while for quantity discrepancy, claim should be filed by the Buyer within 15 days after the arrival of the goods at port of destination. It is understood that the Seller shall not be liable for any discrepancy of the goods shipped due to causes for which the Insurance Company, Shipping Company, other Transportation Organization or Post Office are liable.

11. The Seller shall not be held responsible for failure or delay in delivery of the entire lot or a portion of the goods under this Sales Contract in consequence of any Force Majeure incidents which might occur. Force Majeure as referred to in this contract means unforeseeable, unavoidable and insurmountable objective conditions.

12. Dispute Resolution:

Any dispute arising from or in connection with this Contract shall be submitted to China International Economic and Trade Arbitration Commission for arbitration which shall be trialed in Nanjing and conducted in accordance with the Commission's arbitration rules in effect at the time of applying for arbitration. The arbitral award is final and binding upon both parties.

13. Notices:

All notice shall be written in _____ and served to both parties by fax/e-mail/courier according to the following addresses. If any changes of the addresses occur, one party shall inform the other party of the change of address within _____ days after the change.

14. This Contract is executed in two counterparts each in Chinese and English, each of which shall be deemed equally authentic. This Contract is in _____ copies effective since being signed/sealed by both parties.

The Seller: The Buyer:

Assignment: *Suppose you are Eric Liu, a trade manager of a Tea company. You would like to sign a trade contract with ABC Company. Please write a contract.*

Part V　Cultural Express

Trying Different Jobs vs. Taking a Long Term Career

There is a discussion about young people's career choices. After graduating from university, should young people take several different jobs before taking a long term career? From my point of view, it is not a bad thing to try different jobs when going out into the world. Wise people would benefit a lot from the significant experience of various occupations, and finally head for a successful career.

The most essential reason is that one can make better self-orientation after several jobs. Stepping out of the campus and plugging into the society, young people usually lose themselves. However, an accurate self-orientation is crucial in a career. Trying different jobs will help young people to be aware of their potentials and weakness clearly, and to find his or her own way to compete with others. Many successful people today had engaged in a variety of jobs before they reach their current position. It is a necessary process for one to know oneself, to enrich oneself and to mold oneself through a rich experience of different jobs.

Another advantage of trying different jobs is that it builds up a broad interpersonal relationships. Most of the jobs today require not only professional skills but also the collaboration of different specializations. The experience in your former jobs will teach you how to tackle with people from all walks of life. For instance, in a business, if you had a wide range of human relations, anyone you know in other company or other field may give you a hand, and the crucial information or support offered by them will lead your business to success. In a word, the wide range of people you encounter in various jobs will favor you a lot in your further career.

Admittedly, we cannot deny that beginning with a long term career may have some advantages. In a long term job, one could gain more specialized experience, and will not worry about cases such as losing the position build up in the former jobs. But all of these benefits have a prerequisite, which is one should really fit the job. In this case, trying different jobs first is no doubt a good way toward your most suitable job. It is even suggested that you can start trying different jobs since your college years, like taking various internships that you are interested in.

In conclusion, trying different jobs before taking a long term career is a wise choice. If you can devote yourself to every job and learn from whatever you do, you will develop at a rapid pace and find a promising career in the near future.

拓展词汇

公司部门

Head Office 总公司；Branch Office 分公司；Business Office 营业部；Personnel Department 人事部；Human Resources Department 人力资源部；General Affairs Department 总务部；General Accounting Department 财务部；Sales Department 销售部；International Department 国际部；Advertising Department 广告部；Planning Department 企划部；Research and Development Department (R&D) 研发部；Secretarial Pool 秘书室

公司职务

CEO/GM/President 首席执行官/总经理；Deputy GM/VP/Management Trainee 副总经理；Director 总监；Partner 合伙人；CEO/GM/President Assistant 总裁/总经理助理；Logistics Manager 物流经理；Logistics Supervisor 物流主管；Logistics Specialist/Assistant 物流专员/助理；Purchasing Manager 采购经理；Purchasing Supervisor 采购主管；Purchasing Specialist/Staff 采购员；Trading Manager/Supervisor 外贸/贸易经理/主管；Trading Specialist/Assistant 外贸/贸易专员/助理；Merchandiser Manager 业务跟单经理；Senior Merchandiser 高级业务跟单；Merchandiser 业务跟单；Assistant Merchandiser 助理业务跟单；Warehouse Manager 仓库经理/主管；Warehouse Specialist 仓库管理员；Distribution Manager/Supervisor 运输经理/主管；Customs Specialist 报关员；Documentation Specialist 单证员；Courier 快递员；Warehouse Stock Management 理货员；Creative Artist/Designer 文字/艺术设计人员；Marketing/Advertising Director/VP 市场/广告总监；Marketing Manager 市场/营销经理；Marketing Supervisor 市场/营销主管；Market Analyst/Research Analyst 市场分析/调研人员；CFO/Finance Director/VP 财务总监；Finance Manager 财务经理；Finance

● *Unit 2 Interesting Jobs* ●

Supervisor 财务主管/总账主管；Accounting Manager/Supervisor 会计经理/会计主管；Accountant/Accounting Trainee 会计；Cashier 出纳员；Finance/Accounting Assistant 财务/会计助理；Financial Analysis Manager/Supervisor 财务分析经理/主管；Financial Analyst 财务分析员

职场文具

double sided adhesive tape 双面胶；double sided foam tape 双面海绵胶；batteries for calculator 计算器电池；eraser 橡皮擦；glue 胶水；hard cover book 硬皮抄（笔记本）；hole puncher 打孔机；label 标签；magazine tray 杂志架；marker 记号笔；measure tape 卷尺；name card holder 名片夹；plastic eraser 塑胶橡皮擦；post-it note 便笺纸；rechargeable battery 充电电池；ruler 12" 12 吋尺子；self adhesive tape 透明胶；sharpener 铅笔刀；stapler 订书机；staples 订书钉；steel ruler 12" 12 吋钢尺；super glue 万能胶；tag needle 5"s (standard size) 标准回形针

Unit 3

Business on Campus

Learning Objectives:

You are able to :

☞ Talk about making money on campus

☞ Understand terms in the stock market

☞ Discuss about employment qualities

☞ Write a specification

You are suggested to:

☞ Recognize the English expressions of foreign trade

☞ Be familiar with the procedures to start business on campus

Unit 3　Business on Campus

Part I　Listening and Speaking

Warm-up

Task 1

Directions: Do you know their Chinese meanings? Try to say something about them.

| CV　　credit card　　stock exchange　　diploma　degree　　application letter
bear market　　　　bull market　　graduation ceremony　　job-hunting |

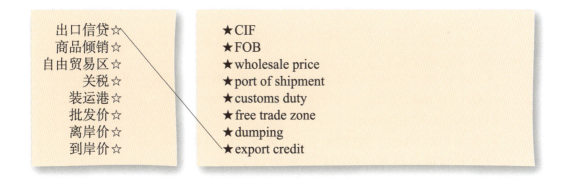

Task 2

Directions: Work with your partner and match the following Chinese phrases with their English equivalents.

出口信贷 ☆　　　　　★CIF
商品倾销 ☆　　　　　★FOB
自由贸易区 ☆　　　　★wholesale price
关税 ☆　　　　　　　★port of shipment
装运港 ☆　　　　　　★customs duty
批发价 ☆　　　　　　★free trade zone
离岸价 ☆　　　　　　★dumping
到岸价 ☆　　　　　　★export credit

Oral Practice

Task 1

Directions: Read the dialogue and answer the following questions.

Talking About Career Choice

You: When was your company founded?
GM: It was founded in 2009.
You: How many employees do you have?
GM: We have over 200 employees in all so far. 60% of them are college graduates.
You: What are your main products?
GM: We manufacture phone accessories.
You: What's your annual output?
GM: The annual output is about 20,000 pieces.
You: Are you developing any new products?
GM: Yes, we are developing a new type of phone charger.
You: How about your R&D department?
GM: We have 3 research labs with ten full-time engineers.

1. When was the company established?
   □ 2009.　　　　　□ 2012.
2. What product do they produce?
   □ Book.　　　　　□ Phone accessories.

Task 2

Directions: Suppose your company wants to expand the business, and create a new position, press officer. Read the following job descriptions and role-play a job interview with your partner. Then reverse roles and do it again.

PRESS OFFICER

($ 22,000 per year)

A leading oil company needs a press officer for its busy office. You should be:

1）Good at making appropriate phone conversations.
2）Excellent at writing reports.
3）Able to go on business trips at least three times a month.
4）Willing to work late several times a week.

48

• *Unit 3 Business on Campus* •

Listening Practice

Task 1

Directions: Listen to the dialogues and tick (√) in the box at the end of the correct answer.

1. How did the woman get to know the job vacancy?
   A. By listening to the radio. ☐
   B. By reading advertisement. ☐
   C. From her head. ☐
2. The woman found the job_____ .
   A. easy to do ☐
   B. easy to get high salary ☐
   C. fit her in her job career ☐
3. What has the woman been doing in South Korea?
   A. As a secretary. ☐
   B. As a teacher. ☐
   C. As a student. ☐
4. What was the woman asked to do in the end?
   A. She was asked to write according to the man's request. ☐
   B. She was asked to write according to the advertisement. ☐
   C. She was asked to wait for the phone call. ☐
5. The interview wouldn't begin until _____.
   A. her applications were well done ☐
   B. her name appeared on the short list ☐
   C. the department head finished signing his name on the applications ☐

Task 2

Directions: In this section you will hear a recorded short passage. The passage will be read three times. You are required to put the missing words or phrases in the numbered blanks according to what you hear.

　　Ladies and Gentlemen,

　　Welcome to you all. We are pleased to have you here to (1)_____ our company. Today, we will first (2)_____ you around our company, and then you will go and see our (3)_____ and research (4)_____ . The research center (5)_____ just a year ago. You may (6)_____ any questions you have during the visit. We will (7)_____ to make your visit (8)_____ and worthwhile.

　　Again, I would like to (9)_____ a warmest welcome to all of you on (10)_____ of our company, and I hope that you will enjoy your stay here.

49

Task 3

Directions: Fill in the blanks while listening to the dialogue and then practise the dialogue in pairs.

> Credit Card Application Form
> Name of User: Mr./Mrs./Miss/Ms _____
> Telephone number: _____
> Profession: _____
> Address: _____
> Any Estate/house: _____ your own
> Car's Make: _____ Monthly Salary: _____
> Date: _____

Part II Reading

Text A

Before Reading:

1. Have you ever thought of starting your own business on campus?
2. Talk with your partner about the advantages and disadvantages of self-employment.

advantages	disadvantages

To Be the Next Millionaire

Facing college graduation in June, Yang Fugang spent most of his days away from campus, managing an online store that sells cosmetics, shampoo and other goods he often buys from local factories. A year and a half ago, like most men in the world, Yang Fugang became bewildered whenever anyone talked about girls' cosmetics. Now he's making a living from them.

Today, his store on Taobao.com—China's fast-growing online shopping bazaar—has 14 employees, two warehouses and piles of cash.

"I never thought I could do this well," said Mr. Yang, 23, who earned $75,000 last year. "I started out selling yoga mats and now I'm selling a lot of makeup and cosmetics. The profits are higher."

Taobao fever has swept Mr. Yang's school, Yiwu Industrial and Commercial College, where administrators say a quarter of its 8,800 students now operate a Taobao shop, often from a dorm room. They were attracted by the idea of Internet selling, and decided to set up their own online shop, with the idea of developing it into a regional shopping site later.

Here in Yiwu, which claims to be the site of the world's biggest wholesale market, Taobao has started to change the look of Yiwu Industrial and Commercial College.

The school's vice dean, Jia Shaohua, points out an area designated as a start-up site for students seeking to get rich. He points to students taking orders by computer, packaging products, sorting inventory and taking photos of the items for display online, and then adds, "Around the school now, there is a whole Taobao Internet supply chain."

Every afternoon, even this summer, when the school should be relatively empty, one can hear the ripping sounds of tape being wrapped around boxes in a building that could pass for a United Parcel Service shipping terminal.

"The students don't need a lot of money," Mr. Jia said. "They just get orders and go find the items at local factories."

Mr. Yang, the cosmetics seller, has become a campus hero. He operates his own warehouses a few miles from the school, in the basements of a pair of residential buildings.

Standing in his crowded warehouse, near boxes of Neutrogena sun block, hairpins, toothbrushes and other cosmetics, Mr. Yang says business could not be better. "Soon, I'll reach $150,000 a month in sales," he said, flashing a big grin.

New Words

(标 ★ 为A级词汇，标 ☆ 为超纲词汇)

graduation	/ˌɡrædʒʊˈeɪʃ(ə)n, -djʊ-/	n.	毕业；毕业典礼
campus	/ˈkæmpəs/	n.	（大学）校园；大学，大学生活
warehouse	/ˈweəhaʊs/	n.	仓库；货栈
industrial	/ɪnˈdʌstrɪə/	adj.	工业的，产业的
★ commercial	/kəˈmɜːʃ(ə)l/	adj.	商业的
administrator	/ədˈmɪnɪstreɪtə/	n.	管理人；行政官
wholesale	/ˈhəʊlseɪl/	n.	批发
designate	/ˈdezɪɡneɪt/	v.	指定；指派
★ chain	/tʃeɪn/	n.	链；束缚；枷锁；连锁
★ terminal	/ˈtɜːmɪn(ə)l/	n.	终点
toothbrush	/ˈtuːθbrʌʃ/	n.	牙刷
grin	/ɡrɪn/	n.	露齿的笑
		v.	露齿而笑，咧着嘴笑

Phrases and Expressions

make a living	赚钱过活；营生；糊口谋生；谋生
set up	建立；准备；安排；引起
a pair of	一对；一双

Exercises

I. Reading Comprehension

Directions: Circle the right answer for the following questions.

1. When did Mr. Yang start his business?
   A. He started his business when he was at college.
   B. He started his business after graduation.
   C. He started his business in high school.
   D. He has never started his business.

2. What products did he sell first?
   A. He sold cosmetics first.
   B. He sold yoga mats first.
   C. He sold both cosmetics and yoga products first.
   D. He sold food products first.

3. Why does online business in Yi Wu become more popular?
   A. Yi Wu has become the site of the world's biggest wholesale market.
   B. Students in Yi Wu have better access to all kind of products.
   C. Students can learn the skills of online business from their classmates and teachers.
   D. All the above mentioned.
4. Which one of the following statements is right according to the school dean?
   A. It is difficult for students to find the items at local factories.
   B. It needs a lot of money to start an online business.
   C. Students do not have to get orders.
   D. A Taobao industrial chain has already formed on campus.
5. Students feel _____ of the growth of online business.
   A. confident   B. difficult   C. dangerous   D. impossible

II. True or False

Directions: Decide whether the following statements are true or false according to the text. Write "T" if the statement is true and "F" if it is false.

_____ 1. Mr.Yang knew everything about cosmetics when he started his business.
_____ 2. There are growing numbers of people operating online shops at TaoBao in Yiwu.
_____ 3. Many students felt it was very difficult to find the items from factories.
_____ 4. School discourages students to start online business.
_____ 5. Mr.Yang ended up with failure in business.

III. Word Usage

Directions: Complete each of the following sentences with the correct form of the italicized word given in the brackets.

1. Thomas was cheerful and _____ (help), and we soon became good friends.
2. The goods that you ordered ten days ago will _____ (deliver) to you tomorrow.
3. Gas prices are _____ (high) here than in other parts of the country.
4. The past decade has seen great economic _____ (develop) in this country.
5. If the engineer _____ (come) here yesterday, the problem would have been solved.
6. While this new law does not _____ (direct) affect the quality of work, it will greatly benefit employees.
7. Now many young people spend several hours a day _____ (talk) on a mobile phone.
8. In China, it is quite _____ (nature) for people to go back home for the Spring Festival.

IV. Blank Filling

Directions: Translate the Chinese part of the following sentences with the correct form of the words and expressions in the box.

graduation	set up	making a living	wholesale
designate	wrap	warehouse	grin

1. He took up writing after _____.(毕业)
2. He _____, delighted at the memory. (咧着嘴笑)
3. The two sides agreed to _____ a commission to investigate claims.(建立)
4. _____ is not that easy for young people.(生存)
5. I stored up the old furniture in the _____.(仓库)
6. You can _____ it up in paper. (包裹)
7. For _____, we offer products at low price.(批发)
8. Please _____ who is to remain.(指定)

V. Translation

Directions: Put the following English sentences into Chinese.

1. Everyone is attracted by beauty and beauty is powerful.
2. Because poor translation might lead up to a misunderstand between the two parties in a business talk, I became more and more anxious about it.
3. He points out they have more knowledge and better tools than his generation had.
4. Your financial outlook could not be better.
5. I suddenly had a dizzy spell and felt as if it was the end of the world.

Text B

Before Reading:

1. What is door-to-door selling? Use your own words to describe it.
2. How do you think about door-to-door selling on campus?

Money Making Schemes

The move-in day is a good time to sell many products to college freshmen, from daily necessities to yearlong passes for tourist spots. Many upperclassmen were allowed to enter dorm building and grab this time to make a fast buck, and more importantly, to acquire early experience in business.

Zeng Renhui, a smart salesperson in Hunan University of Science and Technology, put herself in the freshman's shoes and figured out a new way to sell the SIM (Subscriber Identity Module) cards. Zeng is the administrator of one of the QQ groups of the freshmen in her university. She had been communicating with the freshmen for the whole summer vacation and thus had won their trust. She made full use of the social network she built online and promoted her SIM card business in the QQ group. Zeng has of course created a roaring trade.

Liu Xidan from Northeast Normal University(东北师范大学)applied to be a campus sales agent for the *21st Century,* a weekly magazine, Liu was freed from door-to-door sales, but she still had to deal with challenging situations. Freshmen constantly changed their minds, because of untrustworthy hearsay that people who sold newspapers were all thieves, or another lame excuse. Liu wasn't able to cancel the subscription after issuing the invoice. She was stressed. "You need to be calm, patient and resourceful," said Liu. She kept smiling when facing unfriendly freshmen and patiently shared her personal experiences of reading the Weekly. Liu also sent free sample papers to teachers, who could serve as a credible reference.

Xu Bingchuan is a sophomore at Shan'xi University of Science and Technology. He had an eye for items that would sell well. He chose to sell locks instead of phone cards and newspapers, because it was more difficult to persuade freshmen to pay a hundred to subscribe to a paper for a year, than to spend only several bucks on useful locks. At first, Xu patiently found topics to engage the freshmen in chitchats, but it didn't work well. He met with cold shoulders most of the time. Luckily, Xu had been prepared for the challenge. "My intention was to see how difficult it could be to set up a business," said Xu, who would like a job in marketing or sales after graduation.

Being thick-skinned is necessary for a successful salesperson. Xu held on and adjusted his strategies. He gradually discovered that it's better to be direct with your customers and promote goods from the very beginning.

"Freshmen nowadays are smart. They know your intention and hate hearing you beating about the bush," said Xu. "Being an armchair strategist doesn't work. This is a useful lesson."

New Words

（标★为A级词汇，标☆为超纲词汇）

★ scheme	/skiːm/	n.	计划，方案；体系
necessity	/nəˈsesɪtɪ/	n.	需要；必然性；必需品
buck	/bʌk/	n.	(美)钱，元
★ promote	/prəˈməʊt/	v.	促销
★ agent	/ˈeɪdʒ(ə)nt/	n.	代理人，代理商
lame	/leɪm/	adj.	跛足的；僵痛的；不完全的
patient	/ˈpeɪʃ(ə)nt/	adj.	耐心地；有毅力地
item	/ˈaɪtəm/	n.	条款，项目
persuade	/pəˈsweɪd/	v.	说服，劝说；使某人相信
★ engage	/ɪnˈgeɪdʒ, en-/	v.	吸引或引起(注意、兴趣等)
strategy	/ˈstrætədʒɪ/	n.	战略，策略
smart	/smɑːt/	adj.	聪明的；巧妙的
intention	/ɪnˈtenʃ(ə)n/	n.	意图；目的
hate	/heɪt/	v.	憎恨；厌恶；遗憾
bush	/bʊʃ/	n.	灌木丛

Phrases and Expressions

figure out	解决；弄明白
serve as	充当，担任
instead of	（用……）代替……

Exercises

I. Summary

Directions: Fill in the blanks with the appropriate words according to your understanding.

The first day is a good time to sell many products to（1）_____, from daily necessities to yearlong passes for tourist spots. The sales people are students from（2）_____. They are allowed to enter dorm buildings and know how to（3）_____ their peers quickly. Many upperclassmen grab this time to（4）_____, and more importantly, to acquire early experience in business. Some students sell（5）_____. Some students sell（6）_____. Xu, a student, thought the cheap products were easy to sell, like（7）_____. Being（8）_____ is necessary for a successful salesperson. Xu held on and adjusted his（9）_____. He gradually discovered that it's better to cut loose and promote goods from the very beginning. "Freshmen nowadays are smart. They know your (10)_____ and hate hearing you beating about the bush," said Xu. "Being an armchair strategist (纸上谈兵) does not work. This is a useful lesson."

II. Reading Comprehension

Directions: Circle the right answer for the following questions.

1. When is the best time for upperclassmen to sell products to college freshmen?
   A. The best time is move-in day.
   B. The best time is when they become sophomore.
   C. The best time is when they become juniors.
   D. The best time is when they become seniors.
2. According to Zeng Renhui, what is an efficient way to sell products?
   A. Face-to face communication.
   B. Telephone promotion.
   C. TV promotion.
   D. Social network.
3. After issuing the newspaper invoice, is it possible to cancel the subscription?
   A. Yes.
   B. No.
   C. Not surely.
   D. Not mentioned.
4. According to Xu Bingchuan, what products could be sold well on campus?
   A. Newspaper.
   B. Telephone cards.
   C. Drinks and snacks.
   D. Locks.
5. What does armchair strategist mean?
   A. It means a comfortable chair to rest.
   B. It refers to a very smart way to sell products.
   C. It means idle thinking all day long without doing any practical things.
   D. It is an efficient way to promote oneself.

III. Vocabulary & Structures

Directions: Fill in the blanks with the proper words or expressions in the box.

| allowed to | figure out | deal with | instead of |
| serve as | buck | grab | necessities |

1. People not only need the life _____, but also comfortable life.
2. We make the best out of every _____ we have.
3. Beautiful photographs _____ an excellent source of inspiration for designers.
4. _____ trying to change him, change how you view him.

5. So how do we _____ these new challenges?
6. I _____ a good strategy.
7. This gives us opportunity to _____ market share.
8. The child will not be _____ play outside.

IV. Translation

Directions: Put the following English sentences into Chinese.

1. She still stuck to her point of view no matter how hard I tried to persuade her.
2. Work and life create stress for each of us.
3. Men engage in more high-risk activities than women.
4. He met with cold shoulders most of the time.
5. He beats about the bush for a half hour without coming to the point.

Part III Strategies

翻译解析

　　PRETCO(B)中的翻译题分为两大类：一是句子翻译题，二是短文翻译题。两种题型均是英译汉，其中句子翻译题是选择题，总共有四个选项，选出最恰当的选项，而其他三个选项根据正确性程度，分值为1.5分、1分和0分；短文翻译题是翻译一篇50字左右的英文段落，满分是12分。做这类翻译题要注意句子中关键词、常用句型、固定搭配、习惯用语等，特别注意常用词的一词多义，忠实原文，要符合汉语表达习惯，并在形式、内容上做到统一。

　　要先理解，然后对照选项，细心选择并确定答案。

一、被动句的翻译

　　这类考题较多，对于被动时态翻译考题，考生应经常将被动结构变成主动结构，这样更符合汉语语言特点。同时也要注意一些常用被动句型。

　　【例】2010年6月实考题

　　Many good movies have been produced recently, but I still prefer to watch old movies because they are more interesting.

　　A) 人们对电影是有兴趣的，特别是对老片子，所以我主张放映老片子。
　　B) 近来拍了很多好的影片，既古老又饶有趣味，我觉得人人都喜欢看。
　　C) 近来制作了很多好影片，但是我还是喜欢老片子，因为老片子更有趣。
　　D) 很多好的影片是最近拍的，但我依然觉得过去拍的影片很有意思。

　　这段话是被动态的翻译，movie是被动态的主语，但是这句话其实省略了by people，在翻译过程中，把by people这样的动作执行者主语省略，将英文原句中的主语做宾语，所以这一题C)是最准确答案。

【例】2009年12月实考题

It is widely accepted that the cultural industry has been one of the key industries in developed countries.

A) 发达国家广泛接受,文化是支撑国家工业发展的关键事业。
B) 发达国家已普遍接受,文化产业应看成一种关键性的事业。
C) 大家普遍接受,发达国家应把文化事业看成一种关键产业。
D) 人们普遍认为,文化产业已成为发达国家的一个支柱产业。

这句话中,It is widely accepted that 是固定句型,翻译为"人们普遍认为",the cultural industry has been one of the key industries in developed countries,这句话中,时态是完成时态的被动句,所以最好的答案是D)。相类似的句型还有 It is hoped/reported/said/believed/known that.... 等。

二、长句的翻译

1. 分析句子主干:主语、谓语;确定句子种类:包括主语从句、宾语从句、定语从句、状语从句、同位语从句等。

2. 把握好谓语动词的特点,确定时态、语态、语气等。

【例】2009年6月实考题

Good managers can create an environment in which different opinions are valued and everyone works together for a common goal.

A) 大家一定要齐心协力地工作,创造一个良好的环境,发表各种不同看法。要做好经理。
B) 为了共同的目标,好经理应该尊重各种不同意思,与大家一起工作,创造良好的氛围。
C) 好经理能够创造一种氛围,让不同意见受到重视并且每个人都为共同目标合作奋斗。
D) 为了共同的目标,好经理应该能够提出各种宝贵的意见,为大家创造良好的工作氛围。

这句话中,解题关键要看出 in which different opinions are valued and everyone works together for a common goal 是定语从句修饰 environment,是说明经理要创造什么样的环境,是一个尊重不同意见和大家为共同目标共同努力的环境,所以最佳答案是C)。

【例】2008年6月的翻译段落题目节选

Please take a few moments to complete our customer response form so that we may serve you better in the future.

译文:请抽出几分钟时间来填写反馈信息表,以便我们将来可以更好地为您服务。

这句 so that 表示目的,引导了目的状语从句。

3、注意句子中某些关键词、常用句型、固定搭配、习惯用语等。特别注意常用词的一词多义,尤其是要注意强调句、倒装句、省略句等。

【例】2010年6月实考题

If your company insists on your price, we will have to turn to other suppliers for the goods.

A) 假如贵公司要调整价格,请及早告知我们,以便另做安排。
B) 假如贵公司提高价格,我们不得不从其他地方另寻货源。
C) 如果贵公司不给折扣价,我们不得不采用其他方式购货。

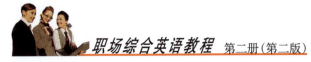

D) 如果贵公司坚持你方报价,我方只能找其他供应商进货。

这句话中,解题关键要看出 turn to 和 insist 的意思,turn to sb.是表示向某人寻求帮助,在这里是表示向别的公司进货,insist是坚持的意思,所以最佳答案是D)。

【例】2009年12月实考题

Not until this week were they aware of the problems with the air-conditioning units in the hotel rooms.

A) 这个星期旅馆里的空调间出问题了,他们没有意识到。

B) 直到这个星期他们才意识到该修理旅馆房间里的空调了。

C) 直到这个星期他们才知道旅馆房间里的空调设备有问题。

D) 他们查不出旅馆房间内空调的故障,这个星期会请人来检查。

这句话中,解题关键要看出这句是倒装句,Not until 表示"……直到……才",且否定词在句首,整句话部分倒装,这句话变成正句序是 They were not aware of the problem with the air-conditioning units in the hotel rooms until this week.所以最佳答案是C)。

练习:

□ All over the world men are searching for new techniques to provide a great deal of housing, inexpensive and quick, for millions of low and middle income families, and especially to meet the urgent housing needs caused by flood and earthquakes.

□ A company in U.S.A. believes it has found one method, houses made of paper. About ten years ago the company supplied a number of the newest paper houses as urgent housing for thousands of farm workers in California. Today, the paper houses are still holding up well. The builders now guess that the houses will have a useful life of at least 15 or 20 years.

Part IV　Applied Writing

Specification (说明书)

说明书,是以应用文体的方式对某事或物来进行相对的详细表述,使人认识、了解到某事或物。说明书要实事求是,不可为达到某种目的而夸大产品的作用和性能。说明书要全面地说明事物,不仅介绍其优点,同时还要清楚地说明应注意的事项和可能产生的问题。说明书可根据情况需要,使用图片、图表等多样的形式,以期达到最好的说明效果。

Sample 1: Read the following medicine specification.

Easy Stomach Tablets Relieve Your Upset Stomach Quickly
Indications: It is effective in the treatment of stomachache resulted from too much eating or drinking
Dosage: 1 tablet every six hours. Do not take more than 6 tablets in 24-hour period.
Storage: Store in tightly sealed containers.
Caution: Not recommended for children under 12 years.

Sample 2: Read the following specification of Clean & Clear Correction Fluid.

SHAKE WELL·TOUCH ON·DO NOT BRUSH
Apply sparingly by dotting the outline of each letter with brush-tip
Allow 8–10 seconds to dry. Recap tightly after each use
Available in colors: white, black, blue
Avoid contact with clothing. Wipe up accidental spills quickly
Caution: The content can be toxic. Non-flammable

Specification Expressions and Sentence Structures

We recommend the user...	我们建议用户……
It can prolong the product life...	这可以延长产品使用寿命……
Its clinical effects include...	临床效果包括……
(be) active/effective against...	对……有效地
In the treatment of all forms of disease...	治疗各种疾病……

Assignment: *Suppose you are from a cell-phone company. Your company recently has developed a new cell-phone. Please write a short cell-phone specification.*

Part V Cultural Express

Tips on Starting an E-Business

Starting an e-business can be a fast and cost-effective way to enter the marketplace and reach a growing pool of potential customers. According to the U.S. Census Bureau, American consumers are increasingly turning to the Internet to locate goods and services, having spent an estimated $133 billion online in 2008—a figure that accounted for 3.3 percent of total sales. Here are a few tips that can help your fledgling web presence turn into a profitable enterprise.

Choose a Strong Name

Choosing the right name for your company is one of the most important decisions you'll make when starting an e-business. Business names like Amazon and Yahoo! have little relation to the products and services offered by their respective companies, however, they share a few common properties: they are short, easy to remember and easy to spell. Those three factors are critical to the success of any e-business, because customers must be able to quickly and easily find your company online. When choosing a name for your e-business, consider how it will look and sound as a domain name. Amazon.com is much easier to remember than Jeff Be zoz Online BookStore.com. Also remember that most customers are used to typing ".com". Domain names that end in ".net", ".biz" or other, lesser-known extensions can cause confusion and appear less trustworthy than their ".com" counterparts.

Invest in Your Website

Your e-business website will serve as your customers' only portal to your company's goods and services, so it's important to make sure that it looks professional and provides customers with the resources needed to research and make purchasing decisions about your products. The cost of hiring a professional web design firm to help you open your virtual doors will vary widely depending on your needs, but this is one area where pinching pennies will hamper your growth.

Just like a bricks-and-mortar storefront should be clean and welcoming, a virtual storefront should showcase a pleasing layout that highlights the most important information and makes navigation simple.

Get Verified

The anonymity of the Internet can hinder a customer's confidence in an unfamiliar company. There are, however, a number of third-party services that specialize in confirming that your e-business is more than just a fly-by-night operation.

Companies like McAfee, TRUSTe and Trust Guard verify your identity and business practices and, if you meet their requirements, provide "trust seals" that you can display on your website to help customers feel more secure about doing business with you. According to e-commerce specialist Dave Taylor, more than 70 percent of online consumers look for trust seals when doing business online.

There are three types of trust seals: security seals, which verify the security of your website and customer data; privacy seals, which certify that your business's privacy policy protects customer information; and identity seals, which certify that there is an identifiable human presence behind the online storefront.

拓展词汇

Love me, love my dog. 爱屋及乌

Seeing is believing. 百闻不如一见

Worse off than some, better off than many; To fall short of the best, but be better than the worst. 比上不足，比下有余

A slow sparrow should make an early start. 笨鸟先飞

white night 不眠之夜

Not pleased by external gains, not saddened by personal losses. 不以物喜，不以己悲

spare no effort; go all out; do one's best 不遗余力

No discord, no concord. 不打不成交

Rob Peter to pay Paul. 拆东墙补西墙

bid farewell to the old and usher in the new; ring out the old year and ring in the new 辞旧迎新

Try first to make their mistake sound less serious and then to reduce it to nothing at all. 大事化小，小事化了

open one's eyes; broaden one's horizon; be an eye-opener 大开眼界

the country flourishes and people live in peace 国泰民安

Going too far is as bad as not going far enough; Beyond is as wrong as falling short; Too much is as bad as too little. 过犹不及

Everything comes to him who waits. 功夫不负有心人

Unit 4

Customer Service

Learning Objectives:

You are able to:
- Make or file a complaint
- Introduce after-sale service
- Understand and respond to customers' complaint
- Comment on customer service
- Write a complaint letter

You are suggested to:
- Identify the English expressions of complaint
- Know successful business strategies

• Unit 4 Customer Service •

Part I Listening and Speaking

Warm-up

Task 1

Directions: Choose the correct English name from the box for each of the following pictures.

| Customer Service Department | Cashier | Warehouse |
| Inquiry Desk | Delivery Service | Reception Desk |

Task 2

Directions: Work with your partner and match the following Chinese phrases with their English equivalents.

总公司 ☆   ★ Executive Secretary
分公司 ☆   ★ Multinational Corporation
人事部 ☆   ★ Quality Control Department
总务部 ☆   ★ Purchasing Department
公共关系部 ☆   ★ Public Relations Department
采购部 ☆   ★ General Affairs Department
质检科 ☆   ★ Personnel Department
跨国公司 ☆   ★ Branch Office
行政秘书 ☆   ★ Head Office

65

Oral Practice

Task 1

Directions: Read the following short conversations between the visitor (V) and the receptionist (R) and then tell your partner what they are talking about and answer the following questions.

R: May I help you?

V: Yes, I am James Mason from Anderson and Associates. I would like to see Mr. Smith.

R: Do you have an appointment?

V: Yes, he knows I am coming. Our meeting is set for 2 o'clock.

R: I wonder if Mr. Smith forgot your meeting, I am afraid he left the office this morning and he is not expected back until after 4 p.m. Let me find out if he made an arrangement for someone else to meet with you in his place. Will you please have a seat?

V: Sure.

R: Yeah, Mr. Mason, I just checked with their office manager Ms. Terry, she said Mr. Smith briefed her on your project and she is just finishing up a meeting now. She should be with you shortly. Would you like me to show you around while you are waiting?

V: That would be very nice, thank you!

R: Right this way Mr. Mason, we can start with our front office, when Ms. Terry is ready, you may take the elevator at the front to the 6th floor. There is a conference room already prepared.

1. When will the meeting be expected to be held?
   ☐ 2 o'clock.   ☐ 3 o'clock.
2. What is Ms. Terry's job?
   ☐ Office manager.   ☐ General manager.
3. Why does Ms. Terry meet Mr. Mason at last?
   ☐ Because Mr. Smith is out and asks Ms. Terry to discuss business with Mr. Mason.
   ☐ Because Ms. Terry is more suited to handle this case.

Task 2

Directions: Read the following conversations and find the themes based on the clues given below.

> do the hotel reception　　　　ask for direction
> explain the delivery service　　ask if there is an access to the Internet
> write a customer satisfaction survey

1. R: What can I do for you?
   V: I want to book a double room.
2. R: Hello, is there anything else that I can help you with?
   V: Yes, I am looking for the laundry room.
3. R: The products would be delivered within 2 days after you place your order.
   V: OK. I will tell our manager about this.
4. R: If you have any problem, please don't hesitate to let me know.
   V: Thanks. Is there an access to the Internet in the room?
5. R: Recently, we are doing a customer satisfaction survey, could you help us fill out the form?
   V: Sure, I'd love to.

Task 3

Directions: Suppose you want to buy a computer, you come to the shop and ask a shop assistant about the computer and the after-sale service. Role-play a conversation with your partner. Then reverse roles and do it again.

> **COMPUTER FOR SALE**
>
> 1 year warranty
>
> Free 24-hour delivery
>
> 14-day money back guarantee
>
> 180 RMB software package free
>
> **Buy now, only RMB 4999 !**
>
> For further information
>
> Please call 6280110 or visit www. 4u.com.cn

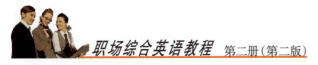

Listening Practice

Task 1

Directions: Listen to the dialogue and tick (√) in the box at the end of the correct answer.

1. The woman welcomed the man to _____.
   A. rental Property Management ☐
   B. manager's office ☐
   C. the centre of Rental Property Management ☐
2. The specific location in the man's mind is _____.
   A. near the hospital ☐
   B. near the swimming pool ☐
   C. near the university ☐
3. The man would like to rent a two-bedroom apartment at the price from _____.
   A. $400 to $500 a month ☐
   B. $400 to $450 a month ☐
   C. $350 to $400 a month ☐
4. The man would like to have _____.
   A. a dishwasher and a swimming pool ☐
   B. a dishwasher, a bathroom and central air ☐
   C. a dishwasher, a washing machine and air conditioner ☐
5. What did the woman suggest the man to do?
   A. She needs a damage deposit of $300. ☐
   B. She needs the deposit of $300 as soon as possible. ☐
   C. She suggests the man look around Broadway. ☐

Task 2

Directions: In this section you will hear a recorded short passage. The passage will be read three times. You are required to put the missing words or phrases in the numbered blanks according to what you hear.

Ladies and gentlemen,

  It's a great (1) _____ to have you visit us today. I'm very happy to have the (2) _____ to (3) _____ our company to you. The company was established in (4) _____. We mainly manufacture electronic goods and (5) _____ them all over the world. Our sales were about (6) _____ last year, and our business is growing steadily.

  We have offices in Asia, (7) _____ and Europe. We have about 1,000 employees, who are actively working to serve the needs of our (8) _____. In order to further develop (9) _____ market, we need your help to promote (促销) our products.

  I (10) _____ doing business with all of you.

  Thank you.

Task 3

Directions: Listen to the conversation and work with your partner to fill in the form given below.

Gree Microwave Oven

Specifications:
Length: 40 cm
Width: 25 cm
Height: 20 cm
Material: _____
Color: _____
Shape: rectangular

Manufacturer: Shenzhou Electronic, Ltd
Guarantee period: _____

Part II Reading

Text A

Before Reading:
Do you think customer service is important? Why?

The Greatest Customer Service Story Ever Told

The following story is fully true. Most importantly, this is AMAZING. When my alarm clock went off at 3:30 this morning, I knew it was going to be a long day. I was catching a 7:00 am flight out of Newark (纽瓦克) to Tampa (坦帕), Florida (佛罗里达), for a lunch business meeting in Clearwater (清水市), then going back to Newark on a 5:00 pm flight, arriving around 8:10 pm, and getting to my apartment by 9:00 pm or so.

I made my flight and got to my lunch meeting. My first meal of the day was that lunch. By the time I got back to the airport, it was close to 4:00 pm. The flight boarded at 4:30 pm, and I knew when I got home, I wouldn't have time to stop for dinner anywhere, and certainly didn't want to get fast food at either airport. When I got on the plane, my stomach was rumbling a bit, and I had visions of a steak in my head.

As I'm a steak lover, I've developed the liking for Morton's Steakhouses (莫顿牛排馆) and if I'm doing business in a city which has one, I'll try to plan a dinner there if I can. I'm a regular customer, and Morton's knows it. They have a spectacular Customer Relations Management (CRM) system in place, as well as a spectacular social media team, and they know when I call from my mobile number who I am, and that I eat at their restaurants regularly.

As we were about to take off, I made a joke and tweeted the following:

I certainly didn't expect anything from that Tweet. It is just an online joke.

I shut off my phone and we took off. Two and a half hours later, we landed at Newark airport. Walking off the plane, I headed towards the area where the drivers wait, as my assistant Meagan had reserved me a car home.

Looking for my driver, I saw my name, waved to him, and started walking towards the gate, like I had done hundreds of times before.

"Um, Mr. Shankman," he said, "There's a surprise for you here."

I turned around and saw the driver was standing next to someone else, who I just assumed was another driver. Then I noticed the "someone else" was in a tuxedo. And he was carrying a Morton's Steakhouse bag.

Alex, from Morton's Steakhouse walked up to me, introduced himself, and handed me a bag. He then told me that he'd heard I was hungry.

I opened the bag. Inside were a porterhouse steak, an order of Colossal Shrimp, Morton's famous bread, two napkins, and silverware.

Hey @Mortons - can you meet me at newark airport with a porterhouse when I land in two hours? K, thanks. :)

Unit 4　Customer Service

New Words

（标★为A级词汇，标☆为超纲词汇）

amazing	/əˈmeɪzɪŋ/	adj.	令人惊异的
board	/bɔːd/	v.	上船（或火车、飞机、公共汽车等）
rumble	/ˈrʌmb(ə)l/	v.	隆隆作响
★vision	/ˈvɪʒ(ə)n/	n.	幻影；想象力
liking	/ˈlaɪkɪŋ/	n.	嗜好
★regular	/ˈreɡjʊlə/	adj.	有规律的，频繁的
			(regulate *v.*; regulation *n.*)
spectacular	/spekˈtækjʊlə/	adj.	惊人的
★assume	/əˈsjuːm/	v.	以为；假设
notice	/ˈnəʊtɪs/	v.	注意到
steakhouse	/ˈsteɪkhaʊs/	n.	牛排餐厅
napkin	/ˈnæpkɪn/	n.	餐巾纸
silverware	/ˈsɪlvəweə(r)/	n.	银器

Phrases and Expressions

take off	（飞机）起飞
head towards	朝……方向走
next to	紧邻；在……近旁

Notes

Morton's Steakhouses	莫顿牛排馆，是美国一家有名的连锁餐厅。
porterhouse steak	上等腰肉牛排
an order of Colossal Shrimp	一份大虾

Exercises

I. Reading Comprehension

Directions: Circle the right answer for the following questions.

1. What does Mr. Shankman do for a living?
   A. He is a businessman.   B. He is a chef.
   C. He likes traveling.   D. He is very fond of steaks.
2. When was the flight to Newark boarded?
   A. 4:30 p.m.   B. 5:30 p.m.
   C. 2:30 p.m.   D. Not mentioned.
3. What can a Customer Relations Management (CRM) system do?
   A. A CRM system effectively ensures a better communication with customers.
   B. From a CRM system, a regular customer can get a better service.
   C. From a CRM system, the customer might also receive the similar good service in other cities.
   D. All of the above.
4. Which one of the following statements is correct according to the text?
   A. Mr. Shankman did not taste steak at last.
   B. Mr. Shankman thinks a CRM system is not so desirable.
   C. Morton's Steakhouses called Mr. Shankman and invited him to eat in their restaurant.
   D. Morton's Steakhouses delivered a delicious meal all the way to the airport.
5. It is _____ for Mr. Shankman to get a bag from Morton's Steakhouses at the airport.
   A. easy   B. difficult   C. surprising   D. impossible

II. True or False

Directions: Decide whether the following statements are true or false according to the text. Write "T" if the statement is true and "F" if it is false.

_____ 1. Mr. Shankman did not like eating streak.
_____ 2. Mr. Shankman posted on the Internet a message that he wanted to eat steak.
_____ 3. Morton's Steakhouses did not see this online message.
_____ 4. Morton's Steakhouses is famous for Chinese food.
_____ 5. Good customer service is very important in business.

III. Word Usage

Directions: Complete each of the following sentences with the correct form of the italicized word given in the brackets.

1. Nowadays, electronic _____ *(pay)* is a more convenient way to pay for purchases than cash and checks.
2. Most of the high school students who _____ *(interview)* yesterday believed that they should continue with their education.

3. According to the survey _____ (conduct) recently, 52% of American business people booked their business travel online last year.
4. The _____ (grow) of online shopping is producing a fundamental change in consumer behavior.
5. The total output of this factory _____ (double) since it was put into operation in 2006.
6. It is the _____ (responsible) of the Human Resources Department to employ new staff members.
7. It was reported that the _____ (injure) people were taken to the hospital immediately after the accident.
8. The bank refused _____ (accept) my application for the loan because they were not convinced by my business plan.

IV. Blank Filling

Directions: Translate the Chinese part of the following sentences with the correct form of words and expressions in the box.

| amazing | liking | take off | head towards |
| leave | regular | apply for | communicate |

1. In our phone interview she told me her _____ story. (有趣的)
2. Certainly he shows little _____ for China and its culture. (喜欢)
3. If you want to retain youthful vigor, you have to take _____ exercise. (周期性的)
4. As our plane _____, I told myself that I would absolutely return someday. (起飞)
5. He _____ the school. (走向)
6. Don't _____ pets in the room while you are out. (留下)
7. I want to _____ this job. (申请)
8. _____ is very important in interpersonal relations. (沟通)

V. Translation

Directions: Put the following English sentences into Chinese.

1. We will land at Taibei Airport in ten minutes.
2. I want to reserve a single room with shower.
3. They assume customers know more than they do.
4. As you like music, you can introduce some famous singers to me.
5. Someone you know may give you a tip that leads you to an astonishing opportunity.

Text B

Before Reading:

What is good customer service? Could you give some examples?

Rules for Good Customer Service

Good customer service is the lifeblood of any business. You can offer promotions and low prices to bring in as many new customers as you want, but unless you can get some of those customers to come back, your business won't be profitable for long. Good customer service is all about bringing customers back, and about sending them away happy—happy enough to pass positive feedback about your business along to others, who may then try the product or service you offer for themselves and in turn become repeat customers. If you truly want to have good customer service, all you have to do is to ensure that your business consistently does these things:

Answer your phone. Make sure that someone is picking up the phone when someone calls your business. Not a fake "recorded robot".

Don't make promises unless you will keep them. If you say, "Your new bedroom furniture will be delivered on Tuesday," make sure it is delivered on Tuesday. Think before you give any promise.

Listen to your customers. Let your customer talk and show him that you are listening by making the appropriate responses, such as suggesting how to solve the problem.

Deal with complaints. If you give the complaint your attention, you may be able to please this one person this one time. Position your business one customer at a time to earn the benefits of good customer service.

Be helpful—even if there's no immediate profit in it. The other day I went into a local watch shop because I had lost the small piece that clips the pieces of my watch band together. When I explained the problem, the owner said that he thought he might have one lying around. He found it, attached it to my watch band—and charged me nothing! Where do you think I'll go when I need a new watch band or even a new watch?

Train your staff to be always helpful,

courteous, and knowledgeable. Talk to them about good customer service and what it is regularly. Most importantly, give every member of your staff enough information and power to make those small customer-pleasing decisions, so he never has to say, "I don't know, but so-and-so will be back at..."

Take the extra step. If someone walks into your store and asks you to help them find something, lead the customer to the item. Better yet, wait and see if he has questions about it, or his further needs. They may not say anything to you at the moment, but when you make an extra effort they will tell other people.

Throw in something extra. Whether it's a coupon for a future discount, additional information on how to use the product, or a genuine smile, people love to get more than they expected.

New Words

（标★为A级词汇,标☆为超纲词汇）

★promotion	/prəˈməʊʃn/	n.	促销,提升,升级;（商品等的）推广
promise	/ˈprɒmɪs/	n.	允诺,许诺
★deliver	/dɪˈlɪvə/	v.	投递;传送 (delivery n.)
appropriate	/əˈprəʊpriət/	adj.	适当的;恰当的
immediate	/ɪˈmiːdiət/	adj.	立即的;即刻的
profit	/ˈprɒfɪt/	n.	收益,得益;利润
★courteous	/ˈkɜːtjəs/	adj.	有礼貌的;谦恭的
knowledgeable	/ˈnɒlɪdʒəb(ə)l/	adj.	了解全面情况的;知识渊博的
extra	/ˈekstrə/	adj.	额外的,补充的,附加的
moment	/ˈməʊm(ə)nt/	n.	瞬间,片刻
coupon	/ˈkuːpɒn/	n.	优惠券
expect	/ɪkˈspekt, ek-/	v.	期望;预料

Phrases and Expressions

pick up	拿起
deal with	应付;对待

Notes

recorded robot: 这里指电话录音。

Exercises

I. Summary

Directions: Fill in the blanks with the appropriate words according to your understanding.

Good customer service is the (1) _____ of any business. Good customer service is all about (2) _____ the customers back. Make sure that someone is (3) _____ the phone when someone calls your business, and don't make promises unless you will (4) _____ them. If you give the (5) _____ your attention, you may be able to please this one person this one time. And let your customer talk and show him that you are listening by making the appropriate (6) _____. Try your best to help the customers even if you can not get (7) _____ at that time. What's more, you should also train your staff to be always (8) _____, (9) _____ and (10) _____.

II. Reading Comprehension

Directions: Circle the right answer for the following questions.

1. What is the lifeblood of any business?
   A. Good customer service.
   B. Bad customer service.
   C. Low price.
   D. Big promotions to customers.

2. Is it wise to get a recorded robot to answer the telephone?
   A. No, it isn't.
   B. Yes, it is OK.
   C. Not mentioned.
   D. Nor surely.

3. What can bring customers back?
   A. A coupon for a future discount.
   B. Staff should always to be helpful.
   C. Staff should deal with one customer at a time.
   D. All of the above.

4. What is not included in "something extra" in the last paragraph?
   A. A coupon for a future discount.
   B. Additional information on how to use the products.
   C. A genuine smile to customers.
   D. An indifferent look upon customers.

5. What is author's attitude to customer service?
   A. Customer service is vital for the development of business.
   B. Customer service is not so important.
   C. Customer service depends on the quality of your products.
   D. Low price and promotions are more important than customer service.

III. Vocabulary & Structures

Directions: Fill in the blanks with the proper words or expressions in the box.

| promotion | pick up | frustrate | extra |
| consistently | make promise | reasonable | discount |

1. His _____ means a raise in salary.
2. _____ the receiver and drop a coin into the slot.
3. I know I _____ you sometimes, but I'll change.
4. What should they do with this _____ income?
5. You should give us _____ for such large quantity.
6. Don't _____ when you are not sure you can do it.
7. This is a policy we have pursued _____.
8. A project should be _____ in every sense, if at all possible.

IV. Translation

Directions: Put the following English sentences into Chinese.

1. In the fall, I tell myself, I will start work and find an apartment and then I'll be a genuine adult.
2. We can deliver what you need to your office.
3. Step back and you will find a good way to solve the problem.
4. The house has a garage attached to it.
5. People like to be around positive people, not energy vampires.

Part III Strategies

写作解析

　　写作题主要考察应用文写作,包括感谢信、道歉信、邀请信、投诉信以及能填写表格,包括电话留言、简历和电子邮件等。这部分分值占总分的15%,作文字数要求不少于80个英语单词。首先要迅速审题,明确自己要表达的内容和写作目的,然后根据题目要求,选择正确的语言形式和风格来表达思想,写完之后,要通读全文,对拼写、语法等方面进行修改,注意保持书写的工整和卷面的整洁。要想拿高分,平时应多模仿范文,掌握应用文写作格式。下面以电子邮件为例说明写作部分解题技巧。

　　电子邮件,也就是我们常说的E-MAIL,随着计算机及互联网的广泛应用,电子邮件已经成为人们日常生活必要的联系方式。它和传统信件相同,均需要填入电子邮箱地址、主题词、正文和尾部落款部分。

【例】2005年12月实考题

说明：根据下列内容写一封电子邮件

发件人：JOHN SMITH（js456@vip.163.com）

收件人：假日酒店（电子邮箱 marketing@expedia.com）

发件时间：12月10号

事由：

1. 因行程改变，取消12月5号以JOHN SMITH的名义在贵酒店预订的12月12号到15号的两个单人房间。
2. 表示歉意，并询问是否需支付违约金。
3. 要求回信确认。

Words for reference：

违约金 cancellation penalty; 假日酒店 Holiday Inn; 以……的名义 in the name of; 确认 confirm

参考范文：

To: Holiday Inn (marketing @ expedia.com)

From: JOHN SMITH（js456@vip.163.com）

Date: Dec.10

Subject: Reservation cancellation

Dear Sir or Madam,

  I am very sorry to inform you owing to the schedule change of our journey we have to cancel our reservation for the two single rooms from Dec.12 to 15 at your hotel under the name of John Smith reserved on Dec 5, 2005. Would you please write us back to confirm the cancellation? And also notify us if there is a cancellation penalty. Thanks very much.

Yours faithfully,
John Smith

【例】2007年6月实考题

说明：假定你是王军。根据以下内容以第一人称发一封电子邮件。

内容：

1. 发件人：王军
2. 收件人：Anna
3. 发件人电子邮件地址：wangjunll007@hotmail.corn
4. 收件人电子邮件地址：annall008@hotmail.com
5. 事由：

  王军在网站www.ebay.com.cn上卖出了一本书，书名《电子商务导论》。买家是美国客户 Anna Brown。

6. 邮件涉及内容：

 1）感谢对方购买《电子商务导论》；

 2）书已寄出，预计一周内到达；

 3）希望收到书后在网站上留下反馈意见；

 4）如果满意，希望向其他客户推荐；

 5）最近还会推出一些新的书，欢迎选购，再次购买可以享受折扣。

Words for reference：

反馈意见 feedback；电子商务导论 Introduction to E-commerce

注意：e-mail 的内容要写成一个段落，不得逐条罗列。

参考范文：

To: Anna Brown (annall008@hotmail.com)

From: Wang Jun（wangjunll007@hotmail.corn）

Subject: Feedback of the transaction

Dear Miss Anna Brown,

　　Thank you very much for buying the book of *Introduction to E-commerce* on the website of www.ebay.com.cn. I have mailed the book and it is due to arrive in a week. I hope you will give your feedback on the website after receiving the book. If you are satisfied with the book, please recommend it to other customers. Soon we are going to put out more new books online and you are more than welcome to check them out. When you make a purchase from us for the second time, you will enjoy a special discount. Thanks again for your business.

Yours faithfully,
Wang Jun

练习：假设你买了一台手提电脑，但是手提电脑有问题，请写一封投诉信来说明问题并提出要求解决问题的条件。

Part IV Applied Writing

Complaint Letter (投诉信)

投诉信是日常生活和日常交往中常见的英文信题材,是对产品或服务表示不满的信件,一般分三个部分:1. 提出投诉内容;2. 说明具体情况;3. 提出解决办法。

投诉信应重点表明投诉的原因,叙事应客观、准确、简洁。最后提出的解决方法应切实可行。在表达自己的不满时,语言要把握分寸,不失风度。

Sample 1

Dear Sir,

I am happy that the refrigerator we ordered last week has arrived on time. But it is a great pity that we find there is something wrong with the refrigerator.

After we used it for several days, we found that food stored in the refrigerating compartment quickly turned bad. When we finally decided to take the temperature in it, we were surprised to find it was around 15℃, far from the standard temperature.

Would you please send a repairman to check on it as soon as possible? I hope that my problem will get your kind consideration.

Yours faithfully,
Li Ming

Sample 2

Dear Mr. Chang,

On September 10, our order for 280 men's cotton sweaters was duly received, but we regret to say that 40 of them in white color were seriously soiled.

We investigated this issue immediately, and the result shows the damage was due to improper packing, for which the suppliers are definitely responsible.

Needless to say, we have suffered a great loss from this, as we cannot sell the sweaters in this condition to our customers. We ask you to conduct an investigation at your end and reply to us as soon as possible.

Sincerely yours,
Li Ming

Unit 4　Customer Service

Expressions for Making a Complaint

complain against sb. about something 投诉……

I am writing to you to complain about 我写信是为了投诉……

I am writing to express my dissatisfaction with 我写信是为了对……表示不满

Please let me know your solution to this matter.
请告知我你将如何处理这件事。

I look forward to receiving a replacement as soon as possible.
我期待着尽快收到调换品。

Assignment: *Suppose you bought a washing machine and later found a worrisome problem. Write a letter of complaint to describe the problem and request a solution.*

Part V　Cultural Express

Wal-Mart Business Culture

Open Door

Our management believes open communication is critical to understanding and meeting our associates' and our customers' needs. Associates can trust and rely on the open door policy; it's one of the most important parts of our culture.

Sundown Rule

Observing the Sundown Rule means we do our best to answer requests by the close of business on the day we receive them. Whether it's a request from a store across the country or a call from down the hall, we do our very best to give each other and our customers same-day service. We do this by combining our efforts and depending upon each other to get things done.

Grass Roots Process

Sam's philosophy lives on today in Walmart's Grass Roots Process, our formal way of capturing associates' ideas, suggestions and concerns.

3 Basic Beliefs & Values

Our unique culture has helped make Walmart one of the world's most admired companies. Since Sam Walton opened Walmart in 1962, our culture has rested on three basic beliefs. We live out these beliefs each day in our interactions with our customers and each other.

10-Foot Rule

The 10-foot Rule is one of our secrets to customer service. During his many store visits, Sam Walton encouraged associates (employees) to take this pledge with him: "I promise that whenever I come within 10 feet of a customer, I will look him in the eye, greet him, and ask if I can help him."

Servant Leadership

Sam Walton believed that effective leaders do not lead from behind their desks. "It's more important than ever that we develop leaders who are servants, who listen to their partners—their associates—in a way that creates wonderful morale to help the whole team accomplish an overall goal," Sam said.

Teamwork

Sam Walton, our founder, believed in the power of teamwork. As our stores grow and the pace of modern life quickens, that philosophy of teamwork has only become more important over the years.

Walmart Cheer

Don't be surprised if you hear our associates shouting this enthusiastically at your local Walmart store. It's our cheer, and while it might not sound serious, we take it seriously. It's one way we show pride in our company.

Associate Stories

Read inspiring stories from associates (employees) that carry out our beliefs and values every day.

拓展词汇

A friendship founded on business is better than business founded on friendship. (John Davision Rockefeller, American businessman)
建立在商务基础上的友谊胜过建立在友谊基础上的商务。（美国实业家 J.D. 洛克菲勒）

Advertising may be described as the science of arresting human intelligence long enough to get money from it. (Leacock Stephen, Canadian economist)
广告可被视为一种长久蒙蔽人类智慧以期从中赚钱的技巧。（加拿大经济学家 L. 斯蒂芬）

All progress is based upon a universal innate desire on the part of every organism to live beyond its income. (Samuel Butler, British writer)
世人莫不怀着一种与生俱来的欲望，要把支出超过收入，此乃一切进步的动力。（英国作家 S. 勃特勒）

Avarice, the spur of industry. (David Hume, British Philosopher)
贪婪是工业的兴奋剂。（英国哲学家 D. 休谟）

Did you ever expect a corporation to have a conscience, when it has no soul to be damned, and no body to be kicked? (Edward Thurlow, British Lawyer)
公司既没有灵魂可以被诅咒，又没有躯体可以被踢翻，难道你指望它有什么良心吗？（英国律师 E. 瑟洛）

For years I thought what was good for our country was good for General Motors, and vice versa. (Charles E. Wilson, former CEO of GM)
多少年来，我始终认为对国家有利的事对我们通用汽车公司也有利，反之亦然。（美国通用汽车公司前任总裁 C.E. 威尔逊）

Good times, bad times, there will always be advertising. In good times people want advertising; in bad times they have to have it. (Bruce Barton British economist)
不管是繁荣时期还是萧条时期，广告总会存在。繁荣时，人们想做广告；萧条时，人们不得不做广告。（英国经济学家 B. 巴顿）

The trouble with the profit system has always been that is highly unprofitable to most people. (E.B.White, American writer)
利润制度的最大弊端始终是绝大多数的人是绝对无利可图的。（美国作家 E.B. 怀特）

There can be no economy where there is no efficiency. (Disraeli, British statesman)
没有效率就没有经济。（英国政治家狄斯雷利）

There is no resting place for an enterprise in a competitive economy. (Alfred P. Sloan, American businessman)
在竞争的经济中，没有企业休息的地方。（美国实业家 A.P. 斯隆）

Unit 5

Culture Shock

Learning Objectives:

You are able to:

☞ Learn to recommend scenic spots to foreigners

☞ Fulfill a Reservation Form

☞ Arrange tours to some scenic spots

☞ Comment on scenic spots

☞ Write a welcome speech/letter

You are suggested to:

☞ Recognize the English expressions of some scenic spots

☞ Be familiar with some traditional Chinese craftwork

• Unit 5   Culture Shock •

Part I   Listening and Speaking

Warm-up

Task 1

Directions: Do you know their Chinese meanings? Try to say something about some of them.

chopsticks	Tangzhuang	Zongzi	folding fans
Chinese Fancy Knots	Taiji	Dragon Boats	Beijing Hutong
Chinese Kongfu	cloisonné vase	Yinyang Sign	

Task 2

Directions: Work with your partner and match the following Chinese phrases with their English equivalents.

边界乐园 ☆	★ Main Street
主街 ☆	★ Adventureland
新奥尔良广场 ☆	★ New Orleans Square
冒险乐园 ☆	★ Frontierland
幻想世界 ☆	★ Critter Country
未来世界 ☆	★ Fantasyland
动物王国 ☆	★ Mickey's Toontown
米奇卡通城 ☆	★ Tomorrowland

Oral Practice

Task 1

Directions: Read the dialogue and answer the following questions.

W: I've heard that those who have been to China buy cloisonné vases as souvenirs. I'd also like to buy some.

M: Our shop is the biggest dealer in the city. Every day we get hundreds of tourists coming in to buy different sizes of cloisonné vases. Please feel free to select from any of them.

W: I'd like a pair of medium-sized cloisonné vases with a light blue background.

M: How do you like this one? The background is pale blue with traditional Chinese paintings of flowers and birds.

W: It's gorgeous. How much is it?

M: One hundred and fifty yuan.

W: Can you come down on the price a little bit?

M: I'm very sorry, madam, but our shop holds a one-price policy. We are not allowed to change the price at will.

W: I see. I'll take a pair then. I am sure my husband will like them.

M: I'm sure he will.

W: Can you pack the vases and send them to the United States for me?

M: Yes, we can. The postage will be an extra charge of one hundred and thirty-eight yuan. There is another extra charge of fifteen yuan for the packing, because we will have to pack them in a special box so that they won't get broken.

W: All right. Here's the money.

M: Can you write down your name and mailing address on this slip?

W: Sure.

1. What would the woman like to buy as souvenirs?
   ☐ Medium-sized cloisonné vases.   ☐ Chinese paintings.
2. Where does the dialogue take place?
   ☐ Bookstore.   ☐ Souvenir shop.
3. How much does one vase cost?
   ☐ One hundred and fifty yuan.
   ☐ One hundred and fifteen yuan.

Task 2

Directions: Suppose you are going to visit HongKong Disneyland. Here is the Park Hours and Calendar for you to read. Role-play a conversation with your partner to discuss your tour schedule. Then reverse roles and do it again.

Daily Calendar

See **park hours**, **fireworks** and **show times**! These times are provided for your reference and may change on the day of your visit. On the day of your visit, please **collect the Times Guide** at Guest Relations for more information about that day's shows, including any revisions to the schedule.

June 5, 2012 (Tuesday)

Park Hours 乐园时间

This is a Standard Day. 10:30AM - 8:00PM

Parade and Firework Times 巡游及烟花表演时间

Flights of Fantasy Parade 迪士尼飞天巡游

Begins in Fantasyland, near the entrance of Storybook Theatre 3:30PM

"Disney in the Stars" Fireworks "星梦奇缘"烟花表演

This spectacular fireworks show transforms the sky above Sleeping Beauty Castle into a stunning evening spectacle 8:00 PM

Special Hours: 个别开放时间
Toy Story Land 反斗奇兵大本营 11:00AM – 5:45PM
Toy Story Land attractions will close approximately 1.5 hours before the fireworks spectacular. Depending on the day's attendance, the closing time of the attractions may be earlier.
Main Street, U.S.A. 美国小镇大街
Animation Academy(动画艺术教室) (Show performs in Cantonese) (以广东话演出) 10:40AM – 7:40PM

Stage Shows 剧场演出

Adventureland 探险世界
"**Festival of the Lion King**" "狮子王庆典"
If you would like to watch the show with simplified Chinese subtitles, please be seated at the last 6 rows. 12:00PM; 2:00PM; 4:30PM; 6:00PM
Fantasyland 幻想世界
"**The Golden Mickeys**" "米奇金奖音乐剧" 12:45PM; 1:45PM; 4:00PM; 5:00PM; 6:15PM
"**Stitch Encounter**" "幸会史迪仔"
Please check for show times in your preferred language (in Cantonese / in Putonghua or in English) at the attraction entrance.
Character Greeting Times 与迪士尼朋友见面
Characters appear occasionally at the following locations, see map for locations:

Main Street, U.S.A 美国小镇大街
Town Square 小镇广场 10:30AM – 4:45PM

Fantasyland 幻想世界
Fantasy Gardens 梦想花园 12:00PM – 6:30PM
Sleeping Beauty Castle 睡公主城堡 10:30AM – 5:30PM
Tomorrowland 明日世界 11:00AM – 5:15PM

• Unit 5   Culture Shock •

Listening Practice

Task 1

Directions: Listen to the dialogues and tick (√) in the box at the end of the correct answer.

1. Where does the tourist come from?
   A. Suzhou. ☐
   B. The Gusu Travel Agency. ☐
   C. America. ☐
2. Where is the tourist visiting in China?
   A. Suzhou. ☐
   B. China. ☐
   C. America. ☐
3. What is the other name of Suzhou?
   A. Beautiful city. ☐
   B. The Venice of the East. ☐
   C. The Oriental Pearl. ☐
4. How many gardens are there in Suzhou?
   A. 150 gardens. ☐
   B. 115 gardens. ☐
   C. 50 gardens. ☐
5. How long will the tourist tour in Suzhou?
   A. One day. ☐
   B. Three days. ☐
   C. A week. ☐

Task 2

Directions: In this section you will hear a recorded short passage. The passage will be read three times. You are required to put the missing words or phrases in the numbered blanks according to what you hear.

Styles of (1) _____, including initial conversations and nonverbal rituals, vary among individuals and (2) _____. The introduction of a university president to a new professor is considerably (3) _____ than that of two people of the same status in the social situation. At a (4) _____, an introduction is likely to be more formal than one made at a party. (5) _____, styles of introductions vary from country to country. Bowing to (6) _____ is customary in parts of the Far East. In the (7) _____ Hemisphere and in other parts of the world, (8) _____ is the common practice. Putting the palm of the hand to (9) _____ is traditional in North Africa. Despite the cultural variations, the purpose of all introductions is always the same—to provide an (10) _____ for people to get to know each other.

Task 3

Directions: Listen to the conversation and work in pairs to fill in the form given below.

Reservation Form:

Name of Guest: Mr./Mrs./Miss/Ms _____
Telephone number: _____
Places to visit: _____
Days for touring: _____
Number of tourists: _____
Date: _____
Price: _____

Part II Reading

Text A

Before Reading:

1. Are you familiar with the following pictures? Have you ever been there? How do you feel about them?

2. Talk with your partner about the differences between Chinese theme parks (主题公园) and Disneyland.

Chinese theme parks	Disneyland

Disney Culture Shock

Before Hong Kong Disneyland opened last year, planners were careful to build the park according to the rules of fengshui. They made sure to serve Chinese food; they also built a garden of costumed characters, since the Chinese like taking photos. However, a free event that was held before the official opening was noisy and overcrowded. Mainland Chinese tourists visiting Hong Kong Disneyland on that day smoked in non-smoking areas, went barefoot and even let children urinate in public. *The Apple Daily* described the behavior of mainland tourists as "disgraceful" while acknowledging that they "brought good business" to the park as it opened its gates on Monday to 16,000 visitors. Meanwhile, local famous stars were offended by rude treatment. Health officials were stopped from entering the park in uniform. Environmentalists protested the shark-fin soup on the menus. This experience raised questions about Disneyland's ability to operate well in this culture. It also raised concerns about what will happen when the company opens its first park on the mainland, in Shanghai, in a few years.

"If they got into trouble in Hong Kong, it is certain they will get into trouble on the mainland." said Chan Kin Man, a professor at the Chinese University of Hong Kong. "Disneyland is a symbol of the West. When relations between the United States and China turn sour, it might turn into a target," Chan said.

Despite several sold-out days over Christmas, Disney was unprepared for the early reaction to a promotion during the Lunar New Year. Hundreds of already ticketed customers were locked out because the park was full. Everything was in disorder: crying children, angry parents and tourists climbing fences to get in.

Disneyland called the problems "growing pains". They found it difficult to move forward since they had a group of people who were fond of anything Western, but they also had a strong group of nationalists. In order to offer a more satisfying service, Hong Kong Disneyland has made changes, and then there were signs of some success.

Huang Xianyi, 50, a bank clerk from mainland China, was among the first to arrive at Hong Kong Disneyland on a recent Sunday. By midmorning, he was waiting in line, watching the shows of "The Hunchback of Notre Dame," "Mulan," "The Little Mermaid" and "Woodpecker", etc.

"I liked the rhythm of the show. Themes ranged from adventure to romance, the adventure stories were exciting and comfortable to watch. It suits both children and adults," Huang said. "All those stories remind me of my childhood." "I don't expect to see many Chinese things in Disneyland."

"They do need to improve communications with the public and make sure that they connect with the local people," added John Ap, a theme park expert.

"Understanding the Chinese market takes time," Ap said. "They can learn a lot from the case in Hong Kong Disneyland. I am certain that they'll be a lot more careful when they go into the mainland China."

New Words

（标★为A级词汇，标☆为超纲词汇）

overcrowded	/ˌəʊvəˈkraʊdɪd/	adj.	过度拥挤的
barefoot	/ˈbeəfʊt/	adj.	赤脚的
☆urinate	/ˈjʊərɪneɪt/	v.	小便
disgraceful	/dɪsˈɡreɪsfʊl, -f(ə)l/	adj.	可耻的
★acknowledge	/əkˈnɒlɪdʒ/	v.	承认（事实、局面等）
offend	/əˈfend/	v.	冒犯
uniform	/ˈjuːnɪfɔːm/	n.	制服
environmentalist	/ɪnˌvaɪrənˈment(ə)lɪst, en-/	n.	环保人士
★protest	/protest/	v.	抗议
reaction	/rɪˈækʃ(ə)n/	n.	反应
disorder	/dɪsˈɔːdə/	n.	混乱
nationalist	/ˈnæʃ(ə)n(ə)lɪst/	n.	民族主义者
rhythm	/ˈrɪð(ə)m/	n.	节奏
★adventure	/ədˈventʃə/	n.	冒险
romance	/rə(ʊ)ˈmæns, ˈrəʊmæns/	n.	浪漫史
communication	/kəmjuːnɪˈkeɪʃ(ə)n/	n.	交通，沟通

Phrases and Expressions

turn sour	变得让人扫兴
growing pains	发展时期（尤指初期）的困难
The Hunchback of Notre Dame	钟楼驼侠
Mulan	花木兰
The Little Mermaid	小美人鱼
Woodpecker	啄木鸟

Exercises

I. Reading Comprehension

Directions: Circle the right answer for the following questions.

1. According to what rules was Hong Kong Disneyland build?
    A. The park was built according to the rules of fengshui.
    B. The park was built according to the rules of Western architecture.
    C. The park was built according to the rules of Hong Kong architecture.
    D. The park was built according to the rules of American architecture.
2. What did *The Apple Daily* think of the behavior of mainland tourists? The paper described it as _____.
    A. overcrowded
    B. disgraceful
    C. rude
    D. successful
3. What questions were raised after Hong Kong Disneyland's first opening?
    A. What will happen when the company opens its first park on the mainland, in Shanghai, in a few years.
    B. Whether Disneyland has the ability to operate well in Chinese culture.
    C. When will Disneyland open in Shanghai.
    D. Whether Disneyland will open on mainland, China.
4. What happened in Disney's promotion during the Lunar New Year?
    A. Hundreds of already ticketed customers were locked out because the park was full.
    B. Everything was in disorder.
    C. There were crying children, angry parents and tourists climbing fences to get in.
    D. All of Above.
5. What does the "growing pains" of Disney refer to?
    A. They found it difficult to move forward.
    B. A group of people were fond of anything Western.
    C. There was a strong group of nationalists.
    D. How to suit both the needs of nationalists and Western-lovers.

II. True or false

Directions: Decide whether the following statements are true or false according to the text. Write "T" if the statement is true and "F" if it is false.

_____ 1. They only serve Chinese food in Hong Kong Disneyland.

_____ 2. Tourists can smoke in non-smoking areas in Disney.

_____ 3. When the relations between the United States and China turn sour, Disney will turn into a bridge to connect two countries.

_____ 4. Disney's "growing pains" means that it is painful to grow bigger and bigger.

_____ 5. Disney needs to improve communications with the public.

III. Word Usage

Directions: Complete each of the following sentences with the correct form of the italicized word given in the brackets.

1. I am always _____ *(care)* when crossing a street.
2. He _____ *(official)* remains head of the government.
3. The place was _____ *(overcrowd)* with tourists.
4. Our city is _____ *(grow)* rapidly.
5. There were too many things in the small _____ *(disorder)* room.
6. That love story is very _____ *(romance)*.
7. His _____ *(react)* was quite unexpected.
8. I yelled at him _____ *(angry)*.

IV. Blank Filling

Directions: Translate the Chinese part of the following sentences with the correct form of the words or expressions in the box.

| according to | get into trouble | turn sour | unprepared for |
| in disorder | be fond of | range from | in public |

1. The prices of these goods _____ several dollars to several hundred dollars. (从……变化到……)
2. We used to play together, live together, complete the education together, _____ together. (闯祸)
3. It's human nature for parents to _____ their children. (钟爱)
4. She was totally _____ this incident. (毫无准备)
5. The meeting finished _____. (一片混乱)
6. File the letters _____ dates. (按照)
7. My hip hop skills will never _____. (不会变差)
8. I'm not used to speaking _____. (当众)

94

V. Translation

Directions: Put the following English sentences into Chinese.

1. Before Hong Kong Disneyland opened last year, planners were careful to build the park according to the rules of fengshui.
2. Environmentalists protested the shark-fin soup on the menus.
3. If they got into trouble in Hong Kong, it is certain they will get into trouble on the mainland.
4. Hundreds of already ticketed customers were locked out because the park was full.
5. Everything was in disorder: crying children, angry parents and tourists climbing fences to get in.

Text B

Before Reading:

1. What is culture shock? Use your own words to describe it, and then give some examples.
2. Do you agree that awareness of cultural differences can bridge the gap of misunderstanding? Why or why not?

How to Handle Business Culture Shock

In our increasingly globalized world, more and more people have to travel to new places and interact with foreigners, as their companies are expanding and developing new business relationships. When dealing with these interactions, whether they will be on brief business trips or visits, or extended stays, it is more important than ever to be aware of the cultural differences and sensitivities of all parties involved in the interaction. If they are overlooked in social interactions, minor cultural blunders can become serious misbehaviors.

When beginning a business relationship with members of another culture, there are some fundamental points to take into consideration in order to avoid misunderstanding and endangering a possible beneficial interaction for both groups.

Do your prospective partners come from a more individualistic or collectivistic society?

This is important because it can affect both the way the other company makes decisions, and the way they view you. Americans tend to be more individualistic and can be perceived as aggressive in their business dealings. Collectivistic societies tend to rely on input from a number of people. Some cultures, such as in most Hispanic societies, wish to get to know their prospective business partners on a more personal level before actually undertaking business with them. In these cultures it is often considered rude or untrustworthy to skip the small-talk and interact on a strictly professional level.

Is structure or flexibility more valued?

Learning how a culture considers time and deadlines can save a lot of confusion and disappointment. While some cultures are very strict about scheduling and structure, others perceive these to be less important than actually achieving their goal. Sometimes it is not a "one-or-another" answer. For the Chinese, punctuality depends on the importance of the occasion and the people they are going to meet.

What kind of communication style is appreciated?

While in some cultures, it is acceptable to strongly express emotions during business dealings; in others, such as with the Japanese, this is considered inappropriate. It is useful to find out what kinds of emotional expression are considered negative by the other culture, in order to avoid unwittingly making a bad impression.

How much formality is appreciated?

It is also important to know how formally people interact in a working environment. To some cultures, relative informality and familiarity among workmates or superiors is acceptable; for others, it is a shocking sign of disrespect and a breaking of personal space. While Latin-based cultures are generally noted for their warm behavior, they generally strictly adhere to rules of social propriety. For instance, they always use the third person when addressing superiors or elders. That is also the case in many Asian cultures such as China, Japan and Korea. The social manner and language make a difference at the cross culture workplace. Attempting to dissuade someone from this practice often results in feelings of discomfort and invasion of space, since familiar speech is frequently kept for family members and close friends only.

In the cross-culture business relationship, keep an open mind, try not to form an opinion about the new culture too soon and develop the cultural awareness. You can thus limit misunderstandings from becoming international business blunders.

Unit 5 Culture Shock

New Words

（标★为A级词汇，标☆为超纲词汇）

☆globalize	/ˈgləʊb(ə)laɪz/	v.	（使）全球化
extended	/ɪkˈstendɪd, ek-/	adj.	扩大的
sensitivity	/ˌsensɪˈtɪvɪtɪ/	n.	敏感
blunder	/ˈblʌndə/	n.	疏忽
misbehavior	/ˌmɪsbɪˈheɪvjə(r)/	n.	不礼貌
endanger	/ɪnˈdeɪn(d)ʒə, en-/	v.	使遭受危险
☆prospective	/prəˈspektɪv/	adj.	预期的
individualistic	/ˌɪndɪvɪdjʊəˈlɪstɪk/	adj.	个人主义的
★collectivistic	/kəˈlektɪvɪztɪk/	adj.	集体主义的
aggressive	/əˈgresɪv/	adj.	侵略的
undertake	/ʌndəˈteɪk/	v.	承担
untrustworthy	/ʌnˈtrʌs(t)wəːðɪ/	adj.	不能信赖的
skip	/skɪp/	v.	略过
☆flexibility	/ˌfleksɪˈbɪlɪtɪ/	n.	灵活性，柔韧性
deadline	/ˈdedlaɪn/	n.	最后期限
confusion	/kənˈfjuːʒ(ə)n/	n.	混乱；困惑
schedule	/ˈʃedjuːl, ˈsked-/	v.	安排
★punctuality	/pʌŋ(k)tʃʊˈælɪtɪ/	n.	严守时间
inappropriate	/ɪnəˈprəʊprɪət/	adj.	不恰当的
negative	/ˈnegətɪv/	adj.	消极的
unwittingly	/ʌnˈwɪtɪŋlɪ/	adv.	不知情地
formality	/fɔːˈmælɪtɪ/	n.	礼节
familiarity	/fəmɪlɪˈærɪtɪ/	n.	通晓；熟悉
superior	/suːˈpɪərɪə, sjuː-/	n.	上级
dissuade	/dɪˈsweɪd/	v.	劝阻
invasion	/ɪnˈveɪʒ(ə)n/	n.	侵犯
awareness	/əˈweənəs/	n.	意识

Phrases and Expressions	
culture shock	文化冲击
interact with	与……相互影响，合作
take into consideration	考虑到
adhere to	坚持
social propriety	社会习俗

Exercises

I. Summary

Directions: Fill in the blanks with the appropriate words according to your understanding.

In the increasingly (1) _____ world, more and more professionals travel to new places and interact with foreign people. The key to avoid (2) _____ in the cross-culture business is to keep an open mind, try not to form an opinion about the new culture too soon, and develop the (3) _____ . You should get to know the following four questions. First, try to judge whether your prospective partners come from a more (4) _____ or (5) _____ society. This is important because it can affect both the way the other company makes decisions, and the way they view you. Second, is structure or (6) _____ more valued? Because learning how a culture perceives time and deadlines saves a lot of (7) _____ and frustration for everyone. Third, what kind of (8) _____ is appreciated? It is useful to find out what kinds of (9) _____ are considered negative by the other culture, in order to avoid unwittingly making a bad impression. Finally, it is also important to know how (10) _____ people interact in a working environment.

II. Reading Comprehension

Directions: Circle the right answer for the following questions.

1. Which statement is false?
   A. Those who are expanding their companies overseas should be aware of the cultural shock.
   B. Those who are developing new business relationships should be aware of the cultural shock.
   C. Those who are having holidays abroad should be aware of the cultural shock.
   D. Only students who are studying English should be aware of the cultural shock.
2. If cultural differences are overlooked in social interactions, what will happen?
   A. Misbehaviors and misunderstandings will occur.
   B. Minor cultural blunders will occur.
   C. People will get annoyed.
   D. Business relationships will get sour.

3. When beginning a business relationship with members of another culture, what should be taken into consideration?
   A. Do your future partners come from a more individualistic or collectivistic society?
   B. Is structure or flexibility more valued?
   C. What kind of communication style and how much formality are appreciated?
   D. All of above.
4. In most Hispanic societies, how do people do business with others?
   A. They skip the small-talk to save time.
   B. They interact on a strictly professional level.
   C. They wish to get to know their business partners on a more personal level before actually undertaking business with them.
   D. They are aggressive in their business dealings.
5. How do Chinese consider time and deadlines?
   A. Chinese don't have deadline.
   B. Chinese punctuality depends on the importance of the occasion and the people they are going to meet.
   C. Chinese are not punctual at all.
   D. Chinese are always late for all occasions.

III. Vocabulary & Structures

Directions: Fill in the blanks with the proper words or expressions in the box.

| adhere to | interact with | deal with | be aware of |
| be involved in | apply to | be noted for | in order to |

1. This nation _____ its economic stability.
2. We breathe _____ live.
3. School regulations _____ every student.
4. We must _____ the open policy.
5. I have some business to _____.
6. However, we all need to _____ the potential risks.
7. Teachers have a limited amount of time to _____ each child.
8. She didn't want to _____ trouble.

IV. Translation

Directions: Put the following English sentences into Chinese.

1. When dealing with these interactions, whether they will be on brief business trips or visits, or extended stays, it is more important than ever to be aware of the cultural differences and sensitivities of all parties involved in the interaction.

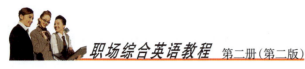

2. Americans tend to be more individualistic and can be perceived as aggressive in their business dealings.
3. For the Chinese, punctuality depends on the importance of the occasion and the people they are going to meet.
4. It is also important to know how formally people interact in a working environment.
5. In the cross-culture business, keep an open mind, try not to form an opinion about the new culture too soon, and develop cultural awareness.

Part III Strategies

阅读解析(一)

在B级阅读理解考试中,Task 1 和Task 2 的题型相同,分别有一小段短文,每段后有5道阅读理解题,每道题后附4个备选答案。在真题试卷中,阅读理解中Task 1 和Task 2 后的题目序号是从36至45排列。

一、识别细节题

在PRETCO(B)阅读理解题 Task 1 和 Task 2 中,识别细节题比较多。做这类题目首先应先将题目浏览一遍,再带着问题看文章,在文章相关内容中寻找所需信息。基本上所有问题的答案都能在文章的相应段落某些句子中直接找到答案。(因为篇幅问题,以下所选的例题中凡是和答题无关的段落和句子基本上全部略去,答案出处的句子皆以下画线标出。)

【例】2009年12月实考题
Task 1
第一自然段中的句子:

Thank you for your interest in Calibre Cassette (盒式录音带) library. <u>This letter tells you about our service. With it we are sending you an application form, so that you can join if you would like to try it.</u>

Calibre library aims to provide the pleasure of reading to anyone who cannot read ordinary print books because of sight problems. We currently have over 7,000 books available for reading for pleasure, including 1,000 especially for children. All our books are recorded cover-to-cover on ordinary cassettes and can be played on any cassette player. <u>They are sent and returned by post, free of charge....</u>

36. According to the first paragraph, the library sends the application form to the readers so that they can _____.
    A) read ordinary books   B) order cassette players
    C) buy Calibre cassette   D) use the library service

　　从该段最后两句话中可以看出,图书馆寄送申请表给读者的目的是让他们加入图书馆并享受其服务。因此该题应选D)。

38. The service of sending and returning books by post is _____.
    A) not available to children   B) paid by the users
    C) free of charge   D) not provided

　　根据内容和句子可以判断出该题答案应为C)。

二、主旨大意题

　　主旨大意题主要考查学生对整篇文章或某一段落大意的理解,要求考生能确定文章的主题(main point)、中心思想(main idea)或给文章拟一个合适的标题(title)。英语短文的主题或中心思想通常在文章的第一句或每小段的第一句表现出来,但也有在文章中间或在文章最后出现的,因此做这种题目常可在这些地方找到与答案有关的信息。

主旨大意题常用的提问句式:
(1) The passage is mainly about _____.
(2) A proper title for this passage would be _____.

【例】2009年12月实考题
Task 1
第一自然段中的句子:
　　Thank you for your interest in Calibre Cassette (盒式录音带) library. This letter tells you about our service...

40. The main purpose of this letter is to _____.
    A) introduce the library's service to readers   B) recommend new books to the readers
    C) send a few catalogues to readers   D) express thanks to the readers

　　在第一自然段中,从第一句和第二句中,就可以直接找到答案,选出A)项。

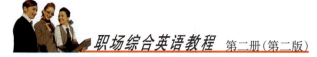

【例】2006年6月实考题

Task 1

第一自然段中的句子：

Unlike Britain, the U.S. does not have a national health care service...

第二自然段中的句子：

In Britain, when people are ill, they usually go to a family doctor first.

...

40. Which of the following would be the best title for this passage?

  A) Types of Doctors in the United States

  B) Healthcare in the United States and Britain

  C) Treatment of Sick Children in the United States

  D) Medical Insurance in the United States and Britain

  所引句子为Task 1的第一自然段第一句和第二段自然中的第一句。从第一段就可以看出B)是正确答案，而第二段第一句更进一步予以证实。

三、逻辑推理题

  逻辑推理题要求考生根据作者的论述，做出一个合乎逻辑的结论。逻辑推理必须建立在文章所提供的事实基础上。考生首先应根据所提问题在文中寻找有关事实，再根据所提供的事实下结论。

必须注意的是：

考生不可根据自己的主观臆断，毫无依据地下结论。

所得结论应符合原文作者的意图。

逻辑推理题常用的提问句式：

From this passage, we can learn that _____.

According to the passage... is important because _____.

To ensure that ... you must _____.

In order to... one should _____.

【例】2009年12月实考题

Task 2

第一自然段中的句子：

  People in some countries cannot use their native language for Web addresses. Neither can

Chinese speakers, who have to rely on pinyin. But last Friday, ICANN, the Web's governing body, approved the use of up to 16 languages for the new system.

42. The approval of the use of 16 languages by ICANN will allow web users to _____.
    A) change their e-mail address
    B) E-mail their messages in characters
    C) have the chance to learn other languages
    D) use addresses in their own language

由引文可判断出,网络主管团体ICANN为新系统正式批准了最多16种语言的使用,而联系前两句话可以推知,此后网络使用者便可以在网址方面使用他们自己的语言了。因此本题应选D)。

第二自然段中的句子:
...The change will also allow the suffix (后缀) to be expressed in 16 other alphabets, including traditional and simplified Chinese characters.

43. The new system will allow the suffix of a Web address to be expressed by_____.
    A) any native language   B) figures and numbers
    C) Chinese characters   D) symbols and signs

本题可使用逻辑推理法,由引文可知,四个选项中除了C),其他三项文中均未提到,故正确选项为C)。

四、判断正误题

做判断题通常使用排除法,即从所提供的四个选项中逐一排除错误选项,剩下的便是正确的;反之,逐一排除正确的,剩下的便是错误的。

判断题常见的提问方式有:
Which of the following statements is TRUE?
According to the passage, which of the following statements is TRUE?
Which statement is NOT TRUE according to the passage?

【例】2007年12月实考题
Task 1
第四自然段中的句子:
Volvo, a famous Swedish carmaker, was the first to use seat belts in 1949. Air bags are also

very important for car safety, because sometimes a seat belt isn't enough. If the car is going really fast and runs into something, seat belts could even hurt the people who wear them.

38. Which of the following statements is TRUE?

    A) People with seat belts fastened will be always safe in cars.

    B) Volvo was the first carmaker to use seat belts in cars.

    C) Air bags will come out before the car hits something.

    D) All cars have air bags in front of the seats.

    由引文可判断出，四个选项中B项是正确答案。

五、判断词义题

这种题目通常要求考生理解一个比较熟悉的词在新语境中的新内涵或者是解释一个不太熟悉的单词或短语。解答这样的题目需要抓住两个线索：词性线索和上下文线索。所谓抓住词性线索就是根据构词法判断词意；所谓上下文线索就是根据单词或短语前后的句子或段落来判断其意思。

判断词义题常用提问方式：

The word ... refers to _____.

The word ... means _____.

The phrase .... Means _____.

【例】2005年1月实考题

Task 1

最后一段：

    Jobs that are suited to telecommuting include writing, design work, computer programming and accounting. If a job involves working with information, a telecommuter can probably do it.

39. The phrase "suited to"(Line 1, Para 3) means _____.

    A) acceptable for   B) difficult for   C) fit for   D) bad for

    根据《基本要求》，suit属于无标记词，即属于在中学阶段就应该掌握的1,000个常用词。它的意思是"适合，恰当"。suited是其过去分词，这里做形容词用，基本意思是"适合的，合适的"。由此我们可以判断suited to 的意思就是fit for，故C)项为正确答案。

【例】2007年6月实考题
Task 2
第二自然段中的句子：

　　This decision was suitable for Los Angeles. <u>The city grew outward instead of upward. Los Angeles never built many tall apartment buildings. Instead, people live in houses with gardens.</u>

42. "The city grew outward instead of upward" means _____.

　　A) the city became more spread out instead of growing taller

　　B) there were few small houses than tall buildings

　　C) rapid development in the city center

　　D) many tall buildings could be found in the city

　　由引文可判断出，四个选项中A)项是正确答案。

Practice
　　Directions: *This part is to test your reading ability. There are 2 tasks for you to fulfill. After reading the following passages, you will find 5 questions. For each question or statement there are 4 choices marked A, B, C and D. You should make the correct choice.*

Task 1
　　Online advertising is the means of selling a product on the Internet. With the arrival of the Internet, the business world has become digitalized (数字化) and people prefer buying things online, which is easier and faster. Online advertising is also known as e-advertising. It offers a great variety of services, which can not be offered by any other way of advertising.

　　One major benefit of online advertising is the immediate spread of information that is not limited by geography or time. Online advertising can be viewed day and night throughout the world. Besides, it reduces the cost and increases the profit of the company.

　　Small businesses especially find online advertising cheap and effective. They can focus on their ideal customers and pay very little for the advertisements.

　　In a word, online advertising is a cheap and effective way of advertising, whose success has so far fully proved its great potential (潜力).

1. According to the first paragraph, buying things online is more _____.
　　A. convenient　　　　B. fashionable　　　C. traditional　　　D. reliable

2. Compared with any other way of advertising, online advertising _____.
　　A. attracts more customers　　　　　　B. displays more samples
　　C. offers more services　　　　　　　　D. makes more profits

3. Which of the following statements is TRUE of online advertising?

   A. It has taken the place of traditional advertising.

   B. It will make the Internet technology more efficient.

   C. It can help sell the latest models of digitalized products.

   D. It can spread information without being limited by time.

4. Who can especially benefit from online advertising?

   A. Local companies.   B. Small businesses.

   C. Government departments.   D. International organizations.

5. This passage is mainly about _____.

   A. the function and the use of the Internet   B. the application of digital technology

   C. the development of small businesses   D. the advantages of online advertising

Task 2

    During our more than 60-year history, with our vast knowledge and experience, Trafalgar has created perfectly designed travel experiences and memories.

    Exceptional value

    Traveling with Trafalgar can save you up to 40% when compared with traveling independently. We can find you the right hotels, restaurants, and our charges include entrance fees, tolls (道路通行费) etc. Because we're the largest touring company with great buying power, we can pass on our savings to you.

    Fast-track entrance

    Traveling with us means no standing in line (排队)at major sights. Trafalgar takes care of all the little details, which means you are always at the front of the line.

    Travel with like-minded friends

    Because we truly are global, you will travel with English-speaking people from around the world, and that leads to life-long friendships.

    Great savings

    We provide many great ways to save money, including Early Payment Discount(折扣), Frequent Traveler Savings and more.

    Fast check-in

    Once your booking has been made, you are advised to check in online at our website and meet your fellow travelers before you leave.

6. Because of its great buying power, Trafalgar _____.

   A. can find the cheapest restaurants   B. can pass on its savings to tourists

   C. takes tourists to anywhere in the world D. allows tourists to travel independently

7. Traveling with Trafalgar, tourists do not have to _____.
   A. bring their passports with them   B. pay for their hotels and meals
   C. stand in line at major sights   D. take their luggage with them
8. Traveling with Trafalgar, tourists may _____.
   A. meet tour guides from different countries
   B. make new friends from around the world
   C. win a special prize offered by the company
   D. have a good chance to learn foreign languages
9. Which of the following is mentioned as a way to earn a discount?
   A. Early payment.   B. Group payment.   C. Office booking.   D. Online booking.
10. After having made the booking, tourists are advised to check in _____.
    A. at the hotels   B. at the airport   C. by telephone   D. on the website

Part IV Applied Writing

Welcome Speech / Letter (欢迎词)

常见的欢迎词分为两大类：一类用于现场口头发表的欢迎词，非正式表达；另一类用于书面表达的欢迎词，正式表达更为郑重。

欢迎词的书面表达特点具有欢愉性，用语简单且具有激情。常常是机关、企事业单位、社会团体等在公共场合欢迎友好团体或个人来访时致辞所用的讲话稿；或者致欢迎信给某人邀请来访。

另一个特点是口语性。欢迎词用于口头表达的常常通俗易懂，令人感到亲切。无论是用于书面发表的欢迎词还是口语欢迎词，最好营造出一种现场感。

格式：

欢迎词的基本格式和写法

1）称呼 attendee

2）开头段 first paragraph（开头通常应说明现场举行的是何种仪式，发言者代表什么人向哪些来宾致欢迎词。）

3）主体（主体部分一般阐述和回顾双方在共同的领域里或事业中的共同立场、观点、目标、原则或具体地介绍来宾在各方面的成就和贡献，指出来宾到访对双方的友谊与合作具有何种现实意义。有些欢迎词也可以介绍本单位的情况让来宾对自己有所了解。）

4）结束语（在结尾处通常要再次对来宾表示欢迎、祝愿和感谢。）

书面欢迎词，一般和写信格式相同：日期、称呼、开头、主体、结束语、致词人头衔和姓名。

Useful Expressions

I welcome you with my whole heart/I offer a warm welcome.

Please permit me to offer you a(n) ... welcome.

We feel honored in offering you a cheerful welcome.

On behalf of..., I am delighted to welcome all of you to...

I'm honored to have this opportunity to welcome all of you to ...

May we bid you a sincere welcome ...?

Sample 1

Dear Guests, Students, Faculty Teachers and Residents,

Please allow me to welcome you sincerely on the occasion of the second anniversary of the founding of the City Polytechnical University. Although it is relatively young for such an institution, it matches itself to older and renowned universities throughout the world.

Within these two years we have developed nine Bachelor's programs, five of which are already successfully running, and seventeen master's programs, in three of which more than fifty students are studying.

Our university publishing house has already printed its first nine editions of our lecturers. We have already developed numerous partnerships with companies from industry and business, and consolidated our collaboration and cooperation with universities from some Asian countries such as China.

We have organized a scientific conference on the occasion of the first anniversary of the university, and it has become a tradition since then.

Last year, a round table on the topic "New Trends and Challenges in Engineering Education" was held. Nineteen students from China, Japan, South Korea took part in the student session, as part of the conference.

As the date of our two-year anniversary has arrived, we can claim to have become a model of the institutional environment of the city. We can help and give it a more academic spirit, and a modern and innovative image. We will keep up this pace and will continue to develop the University. Our goal is for this university to reach the level of the best universities in its academic profile, and to help it become a model of Asian education.

Happy anniversary!

Professor Dalores,
President of City Polytechnical University

Sample 2

Dear New Attendee,

A very good evening to all of you and a warm welcome, as we celebrate the eighth anniversary of our "Lifestyle Magazine". It is an exceptional night. Five years ago Fred and I started this magazine in the garage of a friend's house, because frankly, that was all we could afford as an office. It is thanks to all the special people who joined us here today that we are able to celebrate eight years of not just running this magazine, but being successful at it. To all those people who could not join us here today, we miss you.

Tonight though, is about enjoying ourselves. Not looking at tomorrow but celebrating the present, so go ahead and "let your hair down". Have a magical night! You have all worked so hard for it. Surround yourselves with the happiness you deserve and thank you for making this possible.

Smith White

Assignment: *Suppose you are the Dean of the Chemistry Department. You would like to write a letter to welcome a new teacher (Dr. Johnson) to work with.*

Part V Cultural Express

Cross-Cultural Differences

Meeting people from another culture can be difficult. From the beginning, people may send the wrong signal. Or they may pay no attention to signals from another person who is trying to develop a relationship.

Different cultures emphasize the importance of relationship building to a greater or lesser degree. For example, business in some countries is not possible until there is a relationship of trust. Even with people at work, it is necessary to spend a lot of time in "small talk", usually over a glass of tea, before they do any job. In many European countries—like the UK or France—people find it easier to build up a lasting working relationship at restaurants or cafes rather than at the office.

Talk and silence may also be different in some cultures. I once made a speech in Thailand. I had expected my speech to be a success and start a lively discussion; instead there was an uncomfortable silence. The people present just stared at me and smiled. After getting to know their ways better, I realized that they thought I was talking too much. In my own culture, we express meaning mainly through words, but people there sometimes feel too many words are unnecessary.

Even within Northern Europe, cultural differences can cause serious problems. Certainly, English and German cultures share similar values; however, Germans prefer to get down to business more quickly. We think that they are rude. In fact, this is just because one culture starts discussions and makes decisions more quickly.

People from different parts of the world have different values, and sometimes these values are quite against each other. However, if we can understand them better, a multicultural environment (多元文化环境) will offer a wonderful chance for us to learn from each other.

Travel in China

Regardless of the time spent in advance preparation, you are sure to experience a certain amount of cultural shock when you come to travel in China. The more flexible and sensitive you are to the Chinese culture, the more quickly you will be able to adapt. The best way to know a culture is to touch it, to experience it because each culture has its own reasons to exist, and it is hard to say which one is the standard. Confucius once said, reading and traveling are two main ways to obtain knowledge. It would be great since you want to go to China to see it with your own eyes.

In China, the tour guide and his manager are regarded as the same. Nobody is thought of as a servant, so you have to remember: Don't treat any Chinese, especially your guide as a servant! Tour members frequently make personal requests to their guides, which the guide will try their best to satisfy. Sometimes the guide will consult with your tour leader, and the tour leader will explain to you if they cannot satisfy yours. Generally there is little flexibility in the schedule. Your Chinese guide may go to great lengths to avoid saying "No" to a request. Chinese people like to answer a question in an indirect way, so they would say "We shall consider it" instead of "No".

A smile is indeed the universal language. Joining a group, tourists must understand that the guide needs cooperation from each tourist. Your cooperation will be remembered by your tour leader and guide, as well as other tourists. We do suggest you have the experience, and also wish to listen from you what you see, hear and experience in China. You will have many Chinese friends if you are friendly to them.

拓展词汇

文化

cutural exchange 文化传播；cultural communication 文化交流；international cultural trade 对外文化贸易；international cultural publicity 对外文化宣传；small-fund aid for cultural development 小额文化援助

宗教

Buddhism 佛教；Judaism 犹太教；Islamism 伊斯兰教；Christianity 基督教（总称，基督教包括基督教新教、天主教、东正教）；Protestantism 新教（在中国被称为基督教）；Catholicism 天主教；Orthodox 东正教；Hinduism 印度教；Taoism 道教

景点

the Great Wall 长城；Temple of Heaven 天坛；Hutongs and Courtyards in Beijing 北京胡同；the Grand Canal 大运河；Dujiangyan Irrigation Project 都江堰水利工程；the Terra-cotta Warriors and Horses 兵马俑；Longmen Grottos 龙门石窟；Leshan Giant Buddha 乐山大佛；Jiuzhaigou Valley 九寨沟；Mt. Luhan 庐山；Mt. Huangshan 黄山；Confucius Temple 孔庙；Wuhou Temple 武侯祠；Mt.Taishan 泰山；Mt. Emei 峨眉山；Huanglong Valley 黄龙谷；Yin Ruins 殷墟；Water Town of Tongli 同里水乡；Qiao's Compound 乔家大院；Tengwang Tower 滕王阁；Penglai Pavilion 蓬莱阁；Yellow Crane Tower 黄鹤楼；Lingyin Temple 灵隐寺；Former Residence of Chen Yi 陈毅故居；Lu Xun's Memorial Hall 鲁迅纪念馆

工艺品

porcelain 瓷器；chopsticks 筷子；Chinese fancy knot 中国结；cloisonné 景泰蓝；fan 扇子；silk 丝绸；embroidery 刺绣；New Year Painting 年画；paper cutting 剪纸；festive lantern 花灯；screen tables 屏风；iron picture 铁画；shadow puppet 皮影；puppet 木偶；kite 风筝；diabolo 空竹；windmill 风车；clay figurine 泥人

中国传统节日

Spring Festival 春节
Lantern Festival 元宵节
Qingming Festival 清明节
Dragon Boat Festival 端午节
Water-Sprinkling Festival 泼水节
Seventh Evening Festival 七夕
Mid-Autumn Festival 中秋节

Unit 6

Technology and Life

Learning Objectives:

You are able to:

☞ Talk on the phone

☞ Understand computers and Internet

☞ Follow operating instructions

☞ Write farewell speech/letter

You are suggested to:

☞ Recognize the English expressions of technology

☞ Be familiar with new technological trend

Part I Listening and Speaking

Warm-up

Task 1

Directions: Do you know their Chinese meanings? Try to say something about some of them.

Wi-Fi	GPS	LCD	desktop	laptop
blog	browse	mouse	account	download
e-commerce	virtual	smart phone	text	message
subscriber	nanotechnology	genetic modification		hi-tech

Task 2

Directions: Work with your partner and match the following Chinese phrases with their English equivalents.

超小型设计 ☆
需要一节五号电池 ☆
数字式录音功能 ☆
便携式MP3数字放音机 ☆
嵌入式32兆闪存 ☆
点阵液晶显示歌名 ☆
微型USB PC接口 ☆
智能多媒体插槽 ☆
数字预设均衡器 ☆

★ portable MP3 digital audio player
★ built-in 32MB flash memory
★ smart media card slot
★ super compact slim design
★ digital voice recording function
★ dot-matrix LCD display song title
★ digital preset EQs
★ mini USB PC interface
★ require 1 AA battery

Oral Practice

Task 1

Directions: Read the dialogue and answer the following questions.

Secretary: English Department. Can I help you?
Tom: Good morning. May I speak to Dr. An?
Secretary: One moment, please.
An: Hello, Dr. An here.
Tom: Hello, Dr. An. This is Tom Williams from Miami University.
An: Oh, Tom. You've arrived at Pudong Airport, haven't you?
Tom: Yes, I took the earlier flight.
An: How's your trip?
Tom: Very nice.
An: Would you please wait there and I'll go and pick you up?
Tom: OK. By the way, where will you take me first, the hotel or your department?
An: The hotel, so you can have a little rest first.
Tom: Thank you. Is the hotel far away from your school?
An: No, just a ten-minute walk.
Tom: That's wonderful.
An: See you later.
Tom: See you.

1. Who does Tom want to talk to?
   ☐ Secretary.   ☐ Dr. An.
2. Did Tom arrive early?
   ☐ Yes.   ☐ No.
3. Where will Tom go first?
   ☐ The Hotel.   ☐ The Department.

Task 2

Directions: Imagine a woman is calling Mrs. Sato, but she's not in. You are answering the phone. Role play with your partner according to the clues given in the brackets. Then reverse roles and do it again.

You: （电话铃响了，您拿起电话接听。）
Lady: （向对方询问Mrs. Sato是否在。）
You: （告诉对方她不在，并询问有什么事情需要转告。）
Lady: （让她转告Mrs. Sato给ABC公司回电话，并留下电话号码。）
You: （告诉对方她一回来你就转告她。）
Lady: （表示感谢。）
You: （表示客气。）

Listening Practice

Task 1

Directions: Listen to the dialogue and tick (√) in the box at the end of the correct answer.

1. What can be done when shopping online?
   A. Trying on the clothes you buy.   ☐
   B. Feeling the material you want to buy.   ☐
   C. Buying toys, vegetables and medicines.   ☐
2. What is the interesting question from the anti-online-shopper?
   A. What have you bought online this year?   ☐
   B. When and where do you buy online?   ☐
   C. How do you buy online?   ☐
3. Where does the man buy groceries online?
   A. From Drugstore.com.   ☐
   B. From Homegrocer.com.   ☐
   C. From Amazon.com.   ☐
4. In terms of buying online, the man agrees that shopping online is still _____.
   A. foolish   ☐
   B. complicated   ☐
   C. dangerous   ☐

• Unit 6　Technology and Life •

5. What is the woman's attitude towards online shopping?
   A. Positive.　☐
   B. Negative.　☐
   C. We don't know.　☐

Task 2

Directions: In this section you will hear a recorded short passage. The passage will be read three times. You are required to put the missing words or phrases in the numbered blanks according to what you hear.

Answering Machine (留言机)

　　Answering Machines are very popular in (1) _____ . People use answering machines for two reasons. One is to screen calls(来电显示)and the other is to get phone messages when they are not at (2) _____ .

　　When people (3) _____, they use an answering machine to (4) _____ which calls they will or will not answer. They listen to the message as the caller has left it. When they found out who is calling, they can decide whether to (5) _____ the phone or not.

　　An answering machine can also be used to get a message from someone you want to talk to. The machine takes (6) _____ for you when you are not in and you can (7) _____ it when you get home.

　　Many people (8) _____ when they have to leave messages on answering machines. Sometimes they (9) _____ their messages before they call. This way they are prepared to (10) _____ if a machine answers.

Task 3

Directions: Listen to the conversation and work in pairs to fill in the form given below.

Date _____　　Hour _____
To _____
From _____
Of _____
　　Area Code　　Phone Number
Phone _____　_____
　(　) Telephoned　　(　) Returned Call
　(　) Call Back　　　(　) Will Call Again
　(　) Important　　　(　) Urgent
Message _____
_____
Signed _____

117

Part II Reading

Text A

Before Reading:
1. Can you name some of the advanced technology used in our daily lives?
2. Can you list the advantages and disadvantages of technology?

How Has Technology Changed Our Lives

How technology has changed our lives is certainly one of the easiest questions to answer, because the way technology has influenced our lives is evident in every walk of life. The human mind has achieved everything by the power of imagination. It is by virtue of imagination that man has ushered in an age dominated by revolutionary technological developments.

From the day of landing on the moon to a trip to Mars; from the introduction of Microsoft Windows to the inception of 4G technologies; from tape recorders to Apple iPods; from rarely available landline telephones to abundantly available types of smartphones (智能手机), QWERTY phones (智能键盘手机) and iPhones; from blogging forums to Internet shopping, technological developments have influenced our lives in a way that it is next to impossible to imagine this world without their presence.

Internet technology has changed our life in numerous ways. The global world trade and business has become faster, easier and more reliable. It is easier to book flights and railway tickets. The bill payment and account related works of every business is easily managed by online facilities.

The influence of technology on education is a classic example of how technology has changed our lives. Computers, PowerPoint presentations and Internet technology have given teaching an altogether different dimension.

Education has become computer dominated in this era and it has gone beyond notebooks and blackboards. Computer education has become an integral part of college education all across the globe, as it is the key to make the students competent enough to meet industry requirements.

If you go through the list of latest developments in technology you will find that most of them have revolutionized the way we communicate. Websites like Facebook and Twitter have given birth to the concepts of social media marketing. From business networking to personal online dating,

Unit 6 Technology and Life

communication was never so fast and easy in any century, as it is now.

In the last couple of decades, communication has become amazingly faster, thanks to the Internet that brought email and chatting facilities. Instead of sending letters to their respective destinations, it is easier to send an e-mail to your loved ones.

But we also have to look at some of the negative aspects of technology. Lifestyle habits have changed drastically and nowadays, psychologists are frequently using the term, "Internet addiction" to address certain issues in the lives of people who're constantly glued to their computers. So, if we have to conclude as how technology has changed our lives, then the answer is that it has given us the power to make a difference in our lives by using it wisely. It depends on us, how we use and benefit from it, without getting addicted.

New Words

（标★为A级词汇,标☆为超纲词汇）

influence	/ˈɪnfluəns/	n. /v.	影响,作用
evident	/ˈevɪdənt/	adj.	明显的,显而易见的
imagination	/ɪˌmædʒɪˈneɪʃn/	n.	想象力
★dominate	/ˈdɒmɪneɪt/	v.	控制,操纵
revolutionary	/ˌrevəˈluːʃənəri/	adj.	革命性的
rarely	/ˈreəlɪ/	adv.	很少,难得
blog	/blɒg/	n.	博客
numerous	/ˈnjuːm(ə)rəs/	adj.	数不清的
account	/əˈkaʊnt/	n.	账目,账户
presentation	/ˌprez(ə)nˈteɪʃ(ə)n/	n.	发表,展示,描述
★dimension	/dɪˈmenʃ(ə)n/	n.	规模,范围
integral	/ˈɪntɪgr(ə)l, ɪnˈtegr(ə)l/	adj.	缺一不可的,主要的
★competent	/ˈkɒmpɪt(ə)nt/	adj.	有能力的
drastic	/ˈdrɑːstɪk/	adj.	激烈的,剧烈的
address	/əˈdres/	v.	称呼

Phrases and Expressions

every walk of life	各行各业
usher in	迎来
thanks to	由于
be glued to	（眼睛）紧盯着
benefit from	得益于
get addicted to	上瘾

Proper Names

Facebook	脸谱网
Twitter	推特网

Exercises

I. Reading Comprehension

Directions: Circle the right answer for the following questions.

1. Technology has _____ changed our life.
   A. not   B. completely   C. partially   D. slightly

2. Which gives teaching a different dimension?
   A. Computers.   B. PowerPoint presentations.
   C. Internet technology.   D. All the above.

3. Most of the latest developments in technology have revolutionized the way we _____.
   A. see   B. communicate   C. speak   D. write

4. Which one of the following statements is not true according to the passage?
   A. Technology has impacted every walk of life.
   B. Computer education has become an integral part of college education.
   C. Lifestyle habits haven't changed drastically with the development of technology.
   D. Technology has given us the power to make a difference in our lives by using it wisely.

5. Those who are constantly glued to their computers are called _____.
   A. computer couch   B. net worm
   C. computer fan   D. Internet addict

• Unit 6　Technology and Life •

II. True or false

Directions: Decide whether the following statements are true or false according to the text. Write "T" if the statement is true and "F" if it is false.

_____ 1. How technology has changed our lives is certainly one of the easiest questions to answer.
_____ 2. Career education is the key to make the students competent enough to meet the industry requirements.
_____ 3. Computers have become even smaller and somehow more powerful and faster than ever before.
_____ 4. A few of the developments in technology have revolutionized the way we communicate.
_____ 5. Technology has given us the power to make a difference in our lives.

III. Word Usage

Directions: Complete each of the following sentences with the correct form of the italicized word given in the brackets.

1. A _____ (virtue) state of war exists between the two countries.
2. Several companies are _____ (competent) for the contract.
3. Price tends to _____ (dominant) all other considerations.
4. You will be asked to _____ (presentation) yourself for interview.
5. Maybe I should consult the _____ (account) because my wage is less than last month.
6. The buildings and landscapes are well _____ (integral).
7. A square (正方形) is two-_____ (dimension).
8. He is truly a football _____ (addicted).

IV. Blank Filling

Directions: Translate the Chinese part of the following sentences with the correct form of the words or expressions in the box.

| imagination | evident | available | reliable |
| thanks to | competent | respective | facility |

1. _____ the great performance by all the actors, the play succeeded. (多亏)
2. Tom came down from Beijing for the meeting and Lisa flew from Guangzhou, and when the meeting was over, they returned to their _____ homes. (各自的)
3. Welcome to our hotel. We are fortunate to have this beautiful _____ to accommodate very special guests. (设施)
4. We are looking for someone who is _____ and hardworking. (可靠的)
5. He has no _____. (想象力)
6. I think you are _____ to look after the baby. (胜任)
7. It has now become _____ to us that a mistake has been made. (显然)
8. Further information is _____ on request. (提供)

121

V. Translation

Directions: Put the following English sentences into Chinese.

1. The human mind has achieved everything by the power of imagination.
2. The influence of technology on education is a classic example of how technology has changed our lives.
3. Computer education has become an integral part of college education all across the globe, as it is the key to make the students competent enough to meet the industry requirements.
4. In the last couple of decades, communication has become amazingly faster, thanks to the Internet which brought email and chatting facilities.
5. It depends on us, how we use and benefit from it, without becoming addicted.

Text B

Before Reading:

1. What do you usually do with your mobile phone?
2. What do you know about the iPad? Do you think it is an innovation of communicative technology?

How Did the iPad Change Our Lives?

For iPad owners, their lives must have been changed tremendously after the magic invention was introduced. With the increasing number of people interested in the iPad, people's lives are changing in a positive way.

Why is the iPad so attractive?

For example, last year, when someone enjoys the iPad over coffee in public, there will be a lot of curious people wondering what it was. But today everyone has heard of the iPad. More and more people are enjoying this new, innovative product which is gradually changing their lives.

The Apple iPad was described as a "magical innovative" product. It is! From the sale of more than 1,500 million units within 9 months, it has changed many lives.

Every morning, warmed with a cup of hot coffee, we may take our iPad to view some news from the Internet instead of having to revert to the newspapers or television. We can also write in our blog or reply to e-mails. Unlike the usual way of using the computer, it has become quite easy to use.

It makes our computers extremely jealous. They used to be our most popular office equipment at home, but now, we only think of them when dealing with audio and video material.

Some may say that the iPad is not so useful, for it has no keyboard. Actually, it's quite possible to write articles or blogs with its "virtual" keyboard.

The iPad is also a good resource for the people who do not know how to cook, They can find recipes through the iPad and if utilized properly it can also be a good teaching tool for the kitchen.

Are you feeling tired? Then just listen to some music or play games. The iPad has a large storage capacity for both. It is quite different from the common MP3 players or even the iPod Touch. As for the games, the iPad has made "Plants vs. Zombies (僵尸)" more fun and "Angry Birds" more active! The iPad does add more enjoyment to our daily life.

All the features are included here—news, pictures, games, texts, etc. What's more, we can also enjoy the fun of finger painting on the iPad without all of the mess!

In addition to entertainment, the iPad has changed most people's reading habits. For those who do not like reading paper books, they prefer the iPad eBooks for the joy of changing electronic pages. And thanks to the innovative battery-saving technology, we can enjoy our iPads for many hours.

Believe it or not, the iPad has really changed many aspects of our lives.

New Words

（标★为A级词汇,标☆为超纲词汇）

★tremendously	/trɪˈmendəslɪ/	adv.	惊人地,巨大地
innovative	/ˈɪnɒvətɪv/	adj.	革新的,创新的
★gradually	/ˈɡrædjʊəlɪ/	adv.	逐步地,渐渐地
unit	/ˈjuːnɪt/	n.	个体,一组用具
★virtual	/ˈvɜːtjʊəl/	adj.	虚拟的
recipe	/ˈresəpɪ/	n.	食谱
battery-saving	/ˈbætərɪˈseɪvɪŋ/	adj.	省电的

Phrases and Expressions

revert to	恢复(旧习惯)
as for	至于
in addition to	除了

Proper Names

iPad　　　　　　　　　苹果平板电脑

Exercises

I. Summary

Directions: Fill in the blanks with the appropriate words according to your understanding.

　　Nowadays, almost everyone has heard of (1) _____. It is described as an (2) _____ product. It can be used to (3) _____, (4) _____, (5) _____ and of course, make phone calls. It has no keyboard. But we can write articles with its (6) _____ keyboard. The iPad is also a good (7) _____ for the people who do not know how to (8) _____. Besides, it has a large storage of (9) _____ and (10) _____. Believe it or not, the iPad has really changed our lives.

II. Reading Comprehension

Directions: Circle the right answer for the following questions.

1. The iPad is changing people's life in a _____ way.
   A. bad　　　　　　　B. slight　　　　　　C. partial　　　　　　D. good
2. What does "revert to"(para. 5, line 4) mean?
   A. Return to a former state.　　　　　B. Refer to.
   C. Change into.　　　　　　　　　　D. Ask for.
3. By saying "It makes our computer extremely jealous"(para. 6), we can infer that _____.
   A. the iPad is more beautiful than the computer in appearance
   B. people are tired of using computers
   C. the iPad is more convenient to use than computers
   D. the iPad can totally replace computers
4. According to the text, you can't use the iPad for _____.
   A. viewing news
   B. making phone calls
   C. playing games
   D. reading e-books
5. What's the author's attitude toward the popularization of the iPad?
   A. Indifferent.　　　　B. Sarcastic.　　　　C. Favorable.　　　　D. Pessimistic.

III. Vocabulary & Structures

Directions: Fill in the blanks with the proper words or expressions in the box.

tremendous	innovative	gradually	daily
as for	mess	in addition to	storage

1. _____ the hotel, it was really uncomfortable and miles from the sea.
2. _____ your earlier question, I think we need a second thought.
3. Things _____ changed.
4. _____ the names on the list, there are six other applicants.
5. It makes a _____ change to me.
6. The kitchen is a _____!
7. The Apple is an _____ firm.
8. The machines are inspected _____.

IV. Translation

Directions: Put the following English sentences into Chinese.

1. For the iPad owners, their lives must have been changed tremendously after the coming of this new tool.
2. More and more persons are enjoying this new innovative product which is changing their lives gradually.
3. Every morning, warmed with a cup of hot coffee, we may take the iPad to view some news from the Internet instead of having to revert to the newspapers or television.
4. As for the games, the iPad has made "Plants vs. Zombies" more funny and "Angry Birds" more active!
5. In addition to entertainment, the iPad has changed most people's reading habits.

Part III Strategies

阅读解析（二）

PRETCO(B)中的摘要题主要是识别细节题较多。做这种题目时首先应通读全文,然后根据题目要求寻找所需信息。题干中的有些词就是去文章相应部分寻找的线索。注意答案不能超过3个单词,这就要求我们找到关键词,并剔除与关键词无关的其他词,以确保信息的准确性。

【例】2011年6月实考题

Car Rental (租赁)

Faster Reservation (预订) and Rental Fees

Simply provide your Hertz Club number to speed up the reservation process. And at over 50 locations in the U. S. and Canada, go to Hertz Club Express counters for faster service.

Reduced Rates and Special Offers

Members may receive a special rate on rentals in the U.S., Canada and Europe, and receive a special rate on child seat rentals.

Reserve Specific Brand (品牌) and Model

At 24 major U.S. airport locations, you can choose the brand and model for your weekly and weekend rentals. Only Hertz Club lets you reserve a specific brand and model, like the Ford Mustang. So the car you want is the one you get. Just book your reservation on www. Hertz.com, or by calling 1-800-654-3131.

Car Rental

Way to speed up reservation: by providing your ____46____
Special rates offered to Hertz Club members:
on car rentals in the U. S. , ____47____
on ____48____ rentals
Places for reserving a specific brand and model: at 24 major ____49____
Ways of booking: through the Internet or by ____50____

(1) 通过 reservation 和 providing 这两个关键词,我们可以在 **Faster Reservation** (预订) **and Rental Fees** 部分里找出答案为 Hertz Club number。

(2) 通过 Special rates 和 in the U. S. 这两个关键词我们可以在 **Reduced Rates and Special Offers** 部分找出答案为 Canada and Europe。

(3) 通过 on _____ rentals 我们可以找出答案为 child seat。

(4) 通过 24 major 这两个关键词,我们可以在 **Reserve Specific Brand**(品牌) **and Model** 部分找出答案为 U.S. airport locations。

(5) 通过 by 这个关键词我们可以找出答案为 calling 1-800-654-3131。

• Unit 6　Technology and Life •

Sample 1

The business memo (备忘录) is probably the most frequently used communication within a company. It is called an intra-company communication because it is used by people in their own company or organization. They change to letters, however, when they write a message to people who do not work for their company. A memo creates a written record that may or may not be filed, depending on the receiver and the subject. As you know, spoken messages may be understood or forgotten. A memo, however, becomes a record that does much to ensure the complete communication between the sender and the receiver. The standard form of a memo frequently carries a pre-printed series of items: To, From, Date, and Subject. The first two items include the names of the receiver and the sender. A well-written subject line tells the reader the key topic or topics of the memo.

Business Memo

Function: for communication within a ____1____

Purpose: 1) to keep a ____2____

　　　　　2) to ____3____ the complete communication

Items involved: 1) Receiver

　　　　　　　2) ____4____

　　　　　　　3) Date

　　　　　　　4) ____5____

Sample 2

Dear Sir,

　　I am writing to tell you that your latest shipment(装运) of apples is not up to the standard we expected from you. Many of them are bruised(擦伤), and more than half are covered with little spots. They are classed as Grade A, but I think there must have been some mistake, as they are definitely not Grade A apples.

　　We have always been satisfied with the quality of your produce(农产品), which makes this case all the more puzzling. I would be grateful if you could look into the matter. We would be happy to keep the apples and try to sell them at a reduced price, but in that case we would obviously need a credit(部分退款) from you. Alternatively, you could have us send them back and replace them with apples of the right quality. Would you please call to let me know how you want to handle it?

Yours faithfully,
Fiona Stockton
Purchasing Manager

A Letter of Complaint

Produce involved: Grade A _____1_____

Causes of complaint:
1) many of the apples are bruised
2) more than half of the apples are covered with _____2_____

Suggested solutions:
1) allow to sell at _____3_____ and give _____4_____, or
2) send them back and replace them with apples of _____5_____.

Part IV Applied Writing

Farewell Speech/Letter (欢送词)

欢送词分为两类:一类用于现场口头发表的欢送词;另一类用于书面表达的欢送词。

欢送词的特点主要体现在两个方面:一是惜别的真情流露,二是欢愉、幽默的格调。两者的结合是写好欢送词的关键问题。

欢送词不宜过长。它与欢迎词在分类上大致相同。

欢送词的格式和写法

1) 称呼

2) 开头(说明此时在举行何种欢送仪式,发言人是以什么身份代表什么单位或什么人向宾客表示欢送的。)

3) 主体(主体部分是核心,主要用来回顾双方在访问和合作期间达成了哪些一致意见、取得了哪些突破性进展、合作中取得了哪些成绩、给双方带来了哪些利益。还可以指出双方友谊的性质和价值,双方合作的深远的历史意义等。)欢送词的标题写法与欢迎词大致相同。所不同的是,欢送词可以写得像一篇抒情散文。

4) 结尾

在结尾处再次表示真挚的欢送之情,表达期望再次合作的心愿。

书面欢送词,一般和写信格式相同:日期、称呼、开头、主体、结束语、致词人头衔和姓名。

Useful Expressions

Miss you already. / I miss you already.

See you later. / I'll see you later. / I'll see you later, then.

See you soon. / I'll see you soon. / I'll see you in a little bit.

With all my best thoughts. / With best wishes.

Our visit to China is drawing to a close and we are leaving for Canada shortly.

Thank you for your warm reception and hospitality.

Thanks and best regards.

Bidding you goodbye is really difficult, for you were always a close friend.

We will be keeping in touch, I hope. You can reach me anytime on my phone number or my email.

We really don't know how to thank you. You have been very considerate and helpful.

Sample 1

Good Evening Everyone!

  I am sure all of us know Ms. Sarah Summers in the Sales Department of our office. She has always been an outstanding employee and it is impossible for anyone not to have heard of her yet. Unfortunately, Sarah has chosen to move out of the city to pursue further education. And I, as the head of the sales department, would like to say a few things about her, to her and all of you here, before she leaves.

  Sarah joined our company right out of college. Though our organization was a little hesitant to hire her for her lack of experience, the company also saw true potential in her. And might I add, she never missed an opportunity to prove us wrong. A highly passionate girl, Sarah has, if anything, greatly contributed to the improvement in the function of the sales department.

  Sarah, we are going to miss you deeply, for the liveliness you brought whenever you entered a room. Replacing you is going to be so difficult. I, on behalf of everyone here, wish you all the luck with your life ahead. We hope to see you shine brighter and achieve what you truly deserve.

Sample 2

Dear Mr. Johnson,   Nov. 28

  As you already know, this is my last day with Trade Company. I will be joining Shoe Company on Monday. I'm writing this letter as a token of appreciation for the five wonderful years that I have spent with Trade Company.

  I remember my first day of work. I was so nervous and made a hundred silly mistakes. I was sure you were going to fire me instantly. But instead, you didn't even reprimand（训斥）me. You just pretended that nothing had happened and took upon yourself to make sure that I learned the process thoroughly.

  I cannot thank you enough for showing so much faith in me. Honestly, it was your patience and trust that made me excel in my job here. I've made so many friends

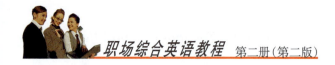

here, whom I'm going to treasure for the rest of my life.

As I leave, my heart is filled with hope, but also with a little regret, on having to part with such a wonderful workplace.

Thank you once again for everything.

Sincerely yours,
_____ (signature)

Assignment: *Suppose you are leaving your company. You would like to write a letter to say goodbye to your workmates.*

Part V Cultural Express

What Is Intercultural Communication?

Intercultural communication is a form of global communication. It is used to describe the wide range of communication problems that naturally appear within an organization made up of individuals from different religious, social, ethnic, and educational backgrounds. Intercultural communication is sometimes used synonymously with cross-cultural communication. In this sense it seeks to understand how people from different countries and cultures act, communicate and perceive the world around them. Many people in intercultural business communication argue that culture determines how individuals encode messages, what media they choose for transmitting them, and the way messages are interpreted. In fact, it studies situations where people from different cultural backgrounds interact. Aside from language, intercultural communication focuses on social attributes, thought patterns, and the cultures of different groups of people. It also involves understanding the different cultures, languages and customs of people from other countries. Intercultural communication plays a role in social sciences such as anthropology, cultural studies, linguistics, psychology and communication studies. Intercultural communication is also referred to as the basis for international businesses.

German or Global?

The CEO of Siemens announced last week that his priority for his second year in charge would be to improve the "global diversity" of managers and warned that Germany's competitiveness could be threatened if it failed to do so.

"The management board are all white males. Our top 600 managers are predominantly white German males. We are too one-dimensional," he said in an interview to mark his first year in charge, according to the *Financial Times*.

He is not alone. Jorma Ollila, while CEO of Nokia, said that his company had to reflect its key markets in the internal diversity of its staff.

Of course, as the FT goes on to point out in its leader, you have to strike a balance. There are many admirable qualities of German companies, such as their reliability and technical prowess; their long-termism, and the consensus between management and workers that has increased competitiveness through wage restraint.

When diversity is encouraged, yet managed and anchored in some common values which everyone understands and shares, it can be powerful indeed. Not just in business, but also in nations.

We have seen how the various "-isms" of the 20th century have resulted in warfare, oppression and economic failure. They have been rooted in the belief that there is an absolute truth or one way of doing things.

The USA, of course, is the prime example of a nation that has achieved economic success by managing to get a truly diverse set of people to stick, on the whole, to some core beliefs—such as that anyone can succeed, that you can take risks without too much fear of failure, and that you can learn from your mistakes. Outside of this set of beliefs, you are encouraged to be different, and diversity is in general respected.

The USA has not been doing well in the global popularity stakes in recent years, and certainly, in politics, the media and in business, one could say that it may have tried to export its way of doing things rather vigorously.

But in Europe, where countries like the UK, Germany, the Netherlands and Belgium are struggling with questions of national identity, we could learn a lot from the Americans. At least they have had a clear and shared sense of purpose, while encouraging and supporting difference.

Getting the balance between diversity and shared values right is vital for business success in a changing world as well.

拓展词汇

科技

emerging industries 新兴产业；Silicon Valley 硅谷；virtual reality 虚拟现实；broadband technology 宽带技术；hypertext transfer protocol(http)超文本传送协议；Wireless Transport Protocol(WTP)无线传输协议；Wireless Application Protocol(WAP)无线应用协议；encryption technology 加密技术；three-dimensional holographic image 三维全息图像；icon 图标；cyber culture 计算机文化；3-D image 三维图像；search engine 搜索引擎；CAD(Computer-Aided Design)计算机辅助设计；CAM(Computer-Aided Manufacturing)计算机辅助制

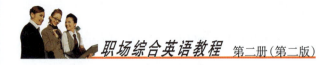

造;networked transaction 网络交易;e-lance economy 电子自由职业经济;e-currency 电子货币;e-commerce 电子商务;hacker 黑客;smart phone 智能电话;integrated circuit 集成电路;Intranet 局域网;cellular communication 蜂窝通信;chip 芯片;netizen 网民;interface 界面;on-line service 在线服务